The Ultimate Soulpreneur Survival Guidebook
Doing what you love, with love, through love, from love
By Ana Ximena Santibañez

Artwork by Laura Emilia Hernandez
Cover & Book design by Ana Ximena Santibañez
©2021 Ana Ximena Santibañez Zamora

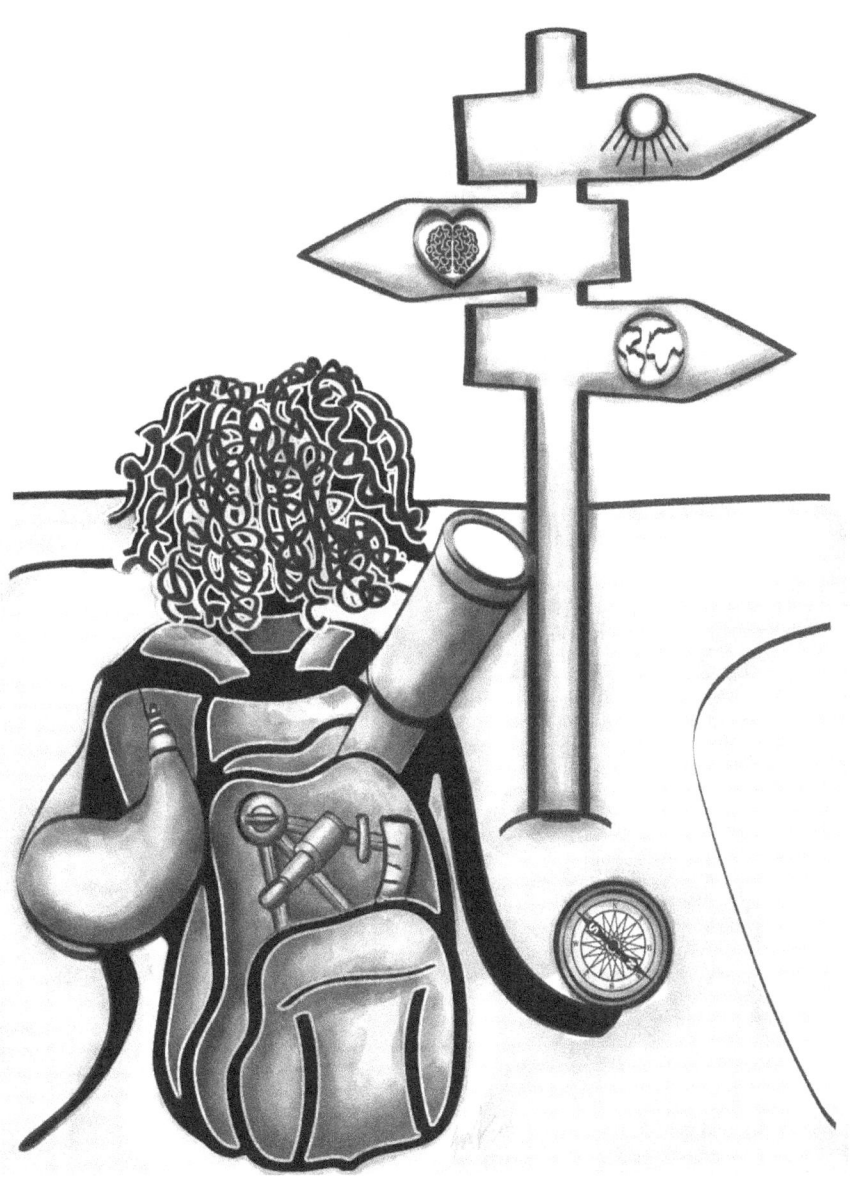

Prologue:

What is a soulpreneur?

A **soulpreneur** is someone who dares and ventures to make a living in alignment with their soul. Heart-centered, whole-hearted, courageous...

Alignment to your soul includes who you are, what you believe, your values, and your belonging in this planet. And not only this planet; the universe, and the whole of creation, but we have to start somewhere, right?

I have to confess that I'm an economist, so I see people and life as a whole as an interaction of activities and exchanges. But, let me be very clear. I do not see activities and exchanges as "utilitarian" activities, but as relationships, as well as personal and community growth experiences.

Take a regular day in anyone's life:

- Exist, exercise or perform a leisure activity, and eat.
- Exchanges with family, friends, and community.
- Perform an activity that will allow myself or someone else from my family unity to generate an income.

For most of the people in the planet, performing that activity that generates income, also known as "work", involves 70 to 90 percent of their waking time and attention. Most people "work for a living", and look forward to the weekend or the nearest holidays to enjoy life. Many others, try to do as much as they can to avoid working: lottery tickets, get rich fast, marry into money, crime, etc.

As a whole, it is considered to live in privilege if you do what you love for a living. Even more so if you can live a financially comfortable life, debt free, owning property, and with freedom to enjoy other activities outside from work. But therein lies a pivotal misconception. Doing something you love, and making a good living out of it should be the rule, not the exception. For that to happen, our approach to work, income, and life must change.

When I decided to entitle this book a "survival guidebook" I really meant it. The way I have chosen to live my professional life, it does take some survival skills. Emotional, financial, physical and mental skills. When my friends approached me to ask questions about living as a freelancer and entrepreneur, I thought it was worth compiling them as a guidebook. This book is the product of those conversations, questions, and the things I wished someone would have shared with me when I struggled.

For the past 20 years, I've worked in over 50 different projects, had 5 different careers (consulting, social researcher, manager, producer, digital content producer, and business coach), and worked in over 10 different industries. "Too unstable" or "what's your area of focus?" some said when I tried corporate jobs. Honestly, my job stability has not lasted more than 2 years with a project or organization because I am simply willing to change, learn, and adapt. I also do not believe my clients should "need me", so once we have both learned what is needed, we just have casual sessions or conversations. But I have long-lasting relationships with clients and associates that go back to my High School projects and organizations.

Now, there is a good reason behind big part of my "job instability". That is because I am willing to fight for what is right, even within systems that were not built for that. It has sadly meant that sometimes I have to quit, or stop a project when it doesn't sit well with my conscience.

I will not allow sexual harassment to be normalized. I cannot endure people disrespecting others just because "they pay their fees" or "they have a contract". I do not believe in nepotism, nor taking a percentage as a commission for something that you've been hired to do—also known as bribery. I demanded my Management professor complain to the book publisher when they claimed corruption was a "standard business practice" in Latin America. And I will not settle for status quo arguments, because the status is always nice and ready to be shaken, shattered, and evolve. I have never endured cheating, hurting others intentionally, or covering up for illegal activities. It hasn't been easy.

Life is sometimes painful, and scary, when you confront wrongdoings. Which, may be one of the reasons why many end up conforming to things that they know are wrong. However, I wouldn't be able to sleep at night if I had done it any other way. Nor could I stand today behind each and every one of these words with full honesty, faith, and the humility that it gives me to know that I always need to practice what I preach.

This is how I came to understand, that I am really what is now described as a **soulpreneur**. A multi-passionate **soulpreneur**. And you know what? That will actually be the future of productive lives as times change. If you don't believe me, then take a look at the top-performing professionals in different industries. It's not about building a product or a career, it's about building a life, and a vision.

In my professional path, I have left projects for many reasons. Because their cycle was over, my values were being challenged, or simply because I learned enough from that experience to implement it in other areas of life or other businesses. My soul, my values and my personal growth have been more important than job stability, career growth, or becoming "the boss".

Again, it has not been easy. It took me roughly 15 years to figure out the best ways to make a decent living, have some work-life balance, and continue to honor my soulful path to success. In the meantime, many of my friends and family kept asking when I was getting a "real job". While everyone got raises, steady monthly income, promotions, and such; I got experience.

Sometimes stepping away from a project felt like a personal failure. Some others, I may have felt betrayed or dismayed. Sometimes projects bloomed and fell apart in just a couple of weeks. Some others, are still going in a different setting or phase. In every case, when things didn't go as I expected, endings were hard. Depression and anxiety are more than a trendy concept. Stress is common when you work for someone else and fulfill their expectations. But when you are your own measure of success, the pain is deeper, and it feels very personal.

I had to find the mental, spiritual, and emotional tools to honor my path, and keep myself alive and safe. I have to say, sometimes those closest to me where the ones who made my non-conventional work-life feel alien and misunderstood even without intending to do so. It is not meanness, they just have not experienced it yet. And when things are so unfamiliar to us, they may seem like a threat.

Then… as it happens these days… Economies crashed, technology changed, industries evolved, and I started getting those emails, and messages, and calls:

"How do you do it?"

"What do I need to know?"

"Can we talk about what you're doing?"

"This happened, and I decided to start my own business/ company/ firm."

"I've always wanted to do this, but I don't know if I can make a living out of it."

"I quit. I couldn't take things anymore. I couldn't compromise my values anymore. Please tell me I'm not crazy for doing it."

Suddenly all those scars became great conversations. Those great conversations, turned into coaching sessions or alliances filled with empathy, inspiration, and encouragement. My experience could guide those I loved, and those I had never met before. I would coach a business owner in the coffee shop near my neighborhood in Mexico City, give an online conference to a Venezuelan school, partner with someone in Costa Rica, Spain, Australia,

London, Los Angeles, and the list kept growing. I noticed that every single lesson learned had been worth it. Even little things that I thought were insignificant allowed me to help, connect, and encourage someone else to stay on their path.

The lessons I've learned are mine. Each individual, our path, our callings, values and passions are unique, diverse and ever changing. But the wisdom I share, can help you walk your own path with commitment, joy, skills, and inspiration. You can do it! Whatever it is, if it's tickling your soul, there is a reason for it. And sometimes it's not about starting a new project or business, but doing what you've been doing all along, but with a new perspective.

Soulpreneurs, in my book, are more than people who start a business aligned with their soul's mission or purpose. They are people who live their lives, and do their jobs in full alignment with their soul. Whether they are scientists, finance professionals, lawyers, prison workers, or animal trainers. Your profession doesn't make a difference. Who you are as a whole human being, does.

I hope this book keeps you company in those dark moments where you don't know what you're doing. That it helps you go back and listen to your heart when the world around you is being too noisy. But mostly, that you will smile at it before you head out to celebrate those amazing moments that are just waiting for you to make them happen. It's a wild ride, but it's so worth it!

Introduction:

I would like to begin with a key concept that, much like a compass, a map, or a GPS, will guide any **soulpreneur**.

Alignment! Aligning our purpose, calling or Divine guidance, with our inner qualities, skills, desires; and last, but not least, with what our community and the world around us may need.

The beautiful thing about alignment, is that when we find it, it's magic! We thrive, grow, learn, and find solutions and opportunities beyond our imagination. When we don't... It's painful. It's dark. Sometimes we lose alignment because the world changes. Sometimes it is because we have changed. But, even in the most positive evolutions, you can struggle to find your new role or position in alignment with your higher purpose, society, your family, etc.

On the bright side, it gets easier to manage all the changes when you know that they are coming, and why they happen. But that is not to say that change, evolution, and success are easy topics. Even if change is hard, it doesn't mean we have to shy away from it.

You will find these at the beginning of each chapter: a little prayer, quote, or mantra for inspiration. There will also be a header image that shows you what elements of alignment are covered in each chapter.

Alignment with Source or Divinity

Alignment with yourself.

Alignment with the planet and community.

You can come back to these chapters when you're struggling with connecting with yourself, divinity/source, or the world.

I want to wrap up this Introduction reflecting on a quote I found as I was wrapping up this book:

> *We know that everything that happens on the outside is a symptom, is a product, is an effect, of something that happened on the inside. Consciousness is the level of cause. Thoughts do matter. Feelings do matter. What happens inside a person does matter. Not only to change in one person's life, but to changing a society.*

-Marianne Williamson,

(The Marianne Williamson Podcast: Conversations that Matter, October 28th, 2020.)

My hope is that you will gain more and more consciousness about yourself and the change that you can bring about. Enjoy life as a **soulpreneur**!

Chapters:

1. There Is Only One of You… A Complex You
2. The Five Biggest Lies About Business and Money
3. Why and How Matter the Most
4. Welcome to The Love Economy
5. There IS Crying in Business
6. New Soul-filled Marketing
7. Collaboration Is Not an Option, It Is A Key to Survival
8. Small Business Does Not Mean Local Business
9. Boundaries and Putting an End to Discrimination
10. Bigger and Better Business
11. Three Reasons to Make Love the Core of Your Business
12. Popularity, Impact, and Transcendence.
13. Let Go of Your Fear and Flow from Love.

1. There Is Only One of You… A Complex You

You are beautiful.

You are perfect.

You are a work of art.

You are a sunrise.

You are the path walked.

You are the light shone.

You are the one.

You are everyone.

May you get to know, love, and trust YOU.

May we all get to witness, enjoy, and learn from the greatness you will display every step of the way.

We need you, we are so thankful you are here. We love you, the one and only, complex you.

I decided to start off this book with this apparently obvious statement. Why? Because every entrepreneur and business owner I have ever met in my life has struggle with this. When you are so passionate, devoted, and decidedly in charge of your business, you tend to forget that you're human.

You are a leaving, breathing, sleeping, and eating person! You are part of a family, a community, and a planet, not just part of the chain of production or economy. You have feelings, ideas, trauma, will, and many other things.

For decades business gurus have tried to tell leaders and business owners to become the most (fill in the blank here). But it just so happens that if you're the most effective, then maybe you're not the happiest. What you really need is to understand that there will always be something you can learn, something you can do better, or even something that you really need to let go and outsource.

So, let's start by reframing and really understanding that:

There is only one of YOU

No matter how hard you try to split yourself into many roles, activities, and relationships, there is only one of you.

If there is something that we have all experienced, especially in times of COVID; it is that our lives aren't as compartmentalized as we thought. When your health, family, job, and all activities in between collide, then there's nowhere to run to.

The truth is that even though you can be a very complex human being, you are only ONE human being. With limited time, energy, ideas, information, space, and resources. In economics we call that "opportunity cost".

What do you give up in order to do something else? Every second you spend working is time you could have used doing literally anything else. Why would you choose to work? Because it's worth it! And the same applies to your leisure time, or family time. Every second you spend in those activities, you could also be doing something else. Why do you choose to do that family dinner? Because it's worth it!

You are your habits and values.

You cannot be a Christian on Sundays, and something else when you vote, or face violence. It's useless to be a Buddhist in the mornings, and go online and spew hate and act from your ego. Life loses sense if you are Sikh, Jewish or Muslim on religious holidays, but then turn your back on your values as you choose how to run your business or take care of your community. And if you can, if you have become accustomed to make the split... Then, you may find that your identity and mental health are struggling. And it's no one's fault but your own.

Our schizophrenic habits of splitting ourselves into too many different people, in order to "fit in", are ruining our lives. Our minds and souls need us to be coherent. Not to mention our communities, relationships, and planet!

When you focus your attention, your energy, and your presence, you notice the difference.

Why is that? When we keep trying to fit in, we stop connecting with our truth. We lose our natural ability to make choices that are aligned with our values. And losing that ability, makes it harder to know what is "right" and "wrong".

On the contrary, if we stand in our truth, and if we are honest with our values and intuition, things are simple. We don't even need to rationalize everything we do, because we are used to acting from a deeper place of knowledge. That inner knowledge -intuition- may help us discern all the noise and misinformation around us. When we live our truth as a habit, we feel more like ourselves.

What does that look like?

Let me share with you a couple of examples:

I care for the environment.

Therefore, I'm mindful of my waste patterns, I care for natural resources, I protect plants and animals. These principles apply to the production of my products and services as well.

Staying healthy is important to me.

Then, I watch what I eat. I exercise, sleep well, and become mindful of how my emotions affect me. But I also apply this when I'm developing my office hours, working conditions, and customer experiences. Staying healthy, applies to me and others.

You are your relationships.

We tend to oversimplify or compartmentalize even our relationships. When you are with your partner or spouse, you may be a woman, wife or lover. But it just so happens, that it doesn't mean that you have stopped being a friend, daughter, or employee in that precise moment.

This has become crucial as we try to split our daily activities while trying to be mothers, teachers, daughters, and just human. Just because our roles and relationships are complex, it doesn't mean that we get extra hours in a day to make them thrive.

Our relationships have duties and activities. They are more than just titles that exist. They are actions that require time and energy. Somehow, modern living made us believe that we could parent, while we worked. Or that we could keep our relationships alive, while not being actively present.

Now, let's clarify this. It does not mean that we cannot fulfill more than one role. It just means we cannot fulfill more than one role at the same time! Your time is limited. The choice of what you do at a specific period of time is one or another. Again... opportunity cost. If you choose to do one thing, you have to let go of another. By the end of this book you're going to love it!

A father can be a great professional, and citizen at the same time. A mother can be a great boss, cook, and friend. But we need to make the time for all those things to happen. And choosing one over the other, means something. We are not just what we "do". We are what we do, why, when, where, how and even who we do it with.

It's worth it to try, and create schedules, chores, and structures that acknowledge that one person cannot be in two different places at the same time. Not because they are not "capable" or "willing", but because there is only one of them.

One mind, one body, and one soul. And it's not just women who have to make the split. Men have struggled with absence in their family environment for centuries!

You are your activities.

When we talk about our activities, we tend to think about our productive activities. We say we are "teachers" or "coaches". We may be "entrepreneurs" or "professionals". That is just what we do "for a living". But we are so much more than that! Even if there is only one of you, one tag or title does not and cannot define you.

You are an artist, a spiritual person or believer, a runner or a kickboxer, a gamer, a music-lover. Then there are your daily activities. You are the one who keeps the house in order. Your spouse could be the one responsible of the cooking, and gardening.

There are many activities in your daily life, that also make you who you are. But not only that, they also take time. Time has become the very limited asset that controls what you are capable of doing. (Throwing in another Economic concept here: scarcity) There are 24 hours in a day, and you need to spread them out in activities that will help you keep relationships, and match your habits and values.

The activities you perform also show the world who you are. Simple things such as greeting people nicely, or treating them politely, make an impact on others. The impression that you give your customer is considerably different. The same happens when you exercise, that makes an impression on your kids and family. If you pray or meditate throughout your day, others will notice it as well. You are your activities! What will you make time for?

You are a complex human being.

That has become clear by now, all the things that make you YOU are not simple. But as a society, it is true as well. We are living complex times where people are trying to make us believe things are easier than they are.

Instead of thinking of ourselves as complex human beings, many have turned us into labels trying to simplify our human experience. That's just false, simplistic, and unfair. No one is just one hashtag. Every human being is a race, nationality, gender, age, generation, etc. Along with a set of skills, occupation, choices, values, trauma, history, relationships, activities, habits, and values.

Now, if you understand the complexity of what makes you YOU, then you understand there are no simple solutions to your problems. There is no magical policy, decision, or person who can change your reality. No guru, coach, or government official who will define your future.

Now, I know that when things get hard, many of us would like to think that magical solution exists. But it is precisely in hard times that we need to see our complexity. Not everything is bad or ruined at the same time. And if it is, then you can start going over all of the things that make your reality what it is, and work on them. Starting with the things you can control, and then trying to influence, little by little, and change the ones that you can't.

Making it easier for each one of us to show up fully.

Each one of us is just an individual person. It seems obvious, but we have not been acting accordingly. Systems and structures are held together as if we were just engaged and connected to them exclusively.

Organizations have schedules, policies, and structures that seem to forget that each one of us is part of a family, community, and also a professional–or a student. Government policies, are being put in place forgetting that individuals have different stories, struggles, wants, needs, and values.

Even health policies are being developed as if everybody acted and reacted in the same way. Yes, it's practical. And it does take more time and resources to go beyond the simple answers. But, again, one of the big lessons of COVID in 2020, is that we NEED to make the time to go beyond simple answers. Our problems are complicated, we can't expect answers to be simple and easy to implement.

Talking about health we need to discuss what we eat, our lifestyle, our age and location, our social and economic class. All of those elements affect whether we get sick or have a resilient body to face sickness. Insurance policies have taken this into account for years, but have we all?

Tough choices may always come for all of us. But we do need to remember, as we try to find what's best for all of us, that one person is many things.

You are a daughter, mother, friend, coworker, citizen, client, owner, believer, revolutionary, and everything in between. You are complex, with all of these things inside of you, but there is only one of YOU.

Recommended clip: "The Revolutionary Power of Diverse Thought",

TED talk by Elif Shafak.

2. The Five Biggest Lies About Business and Money

You are value

You are valued

What you make with your hands

What comes out of your mind

Your presence

You are value

Be grateful and honored by the gifts you give,

and those you receive.

You see and find and enjoy value everywhere you go.

You create, share, and add value through your existence.

We got started with a basic and essential truth. But, the reason why I keep writing books, blogposts, and generating content to share my experience is to stop the lies! I majored in Business and Economics. I know the principles, and I've seen many ways to put them into practice. I know how flexible, playful, and creative a business owner can be.

Yet, I keep seeing terror stories about CEOs, transnational corporations and even the little shop in the corner. Stories about inhuman schedules, low pay, corruption, exploitation, fraud, sexual harassment, and many other problems. They are real. I'm not naïve, but I'm hopeful, because I've seen better. I know it's not business, or capitalism, that is to blame. People and our lack of principles, courage, empathy, awareness, and determination are to blame.

You could create the love child economic system of Marx and Moore, and Jesus; and still have manipulation, misery, pollution, and wars. It's not the system, it's us!

We could talk about many lies about business and money that people keep assuming as true. Time goes by, and some people think that some principles are carved in stone. They don't account for change. We are not the same as we were in the 1900s. There is no such thing as "local" anymore. The "butterfly effect" has gone beyond anyone's control, and change just keeps getting faster and faster.

In all honesty, we have all witnessed changes in the business environment from the Industrial Revolution to the Digital Revolution. We all know this, but not everyone has adjusted their practices and beliefs to it.

Some people know too well that they've been holding on to all these lies about business as true. It may be pure evil and greed. But honestly, sometimes they just don't know how to operate with new mindsets and changes. They cling on to what worked for them, and what seems familiar. But familiar, and "business as usual" is more and more stale and obsolete.

This is why YOU don't think "business as usual" works for you. And it's good! You are here to operate in a totally different system. Your software has been upgraded. You cannot pour new wine into old wine skins. You are here maybe even to create new systems!

We'll uncover each one of those old lies, and at the end of this chapter, you will also find a little checklist that can help you see them in YOUR professional life. It doesn't matter if you work for a big corporation, or you're trying to figure out what to do for a living, it will help you find your way to become part of the business world and make money. Not the dirty feel-guilty greedy kind of money. But...

The "I'm so happy" everything-flows, good-for-all kind of money.

The lies:

1. You have to work to make money.

2. Some careers don't make money.

3. Successful business people are cold-hearted and insensitive.

4. The number 1 focus of a successful business is profit.

5. The customer is always right.

Let's tackle them!

1. You have to work to make money

The truth is you have to be productive and add value to something or someone in order to earn money.

Working has become such a machine-based purpose for people! Under this new umbrella of value, your knowledge, skills, talents, experience, company, and anything that can bring value to others can be compensated. Therefore, you can make money in a positive way!

Now it's not all roses, and laying on the beach or making a million out of your first idea. Don't be fooled or sucked into the "easy money" mentality. You may have to still work those extra-hours, or have some stress days in your life, but your purpose and humanity are connected here. As you'll read in the next chapter, it's not what you do, but why you do it that matters.

2. Some careers don't make money.

This is the reason why everyone in the world has been told that they should be a doctor or a lawyer. Or maybe an accountant or engineer to add into the mix.

This would make it seem as if everything in life had to do with being sick, injured, fighting, making numbers work, or operating a machine. But just ask yourself: "Is that all human beings are and need?"

If that were true, why is it that Hollywood and social media are really the most profitable industries? They are industries based on ideas, dreams, illusions, artistry, creation, imagination, etc. They are not perfect, but they sure can be profitable!

However, we do need to make a point here. If you love doing something and you're good at it, but you're not making money through it, it's just a hobby! It doesn't have to be the one thing you do all your life. It doesn't have to become your source of income. It can become a business, but you need to understand the value that you're adding through it. And be willing to fight for it!

Healing is a service. Entertainment is a service. Knowledge is an asset. Don't just give them away all the time!

That passion project that you have in mind, may not be exactly your business. Maybe you are part of a team that can turn it into one. You may have the idea, and part of the process and someone else could handle the numbers, or the technical side. Or perhaps your idea doesn't work exactly as you envisioned it. Maybe you're not going to be a pop-star, but someone who leads creative therapy sessions by helping others compose or sing!

Your dream, talent, and skills, can be useful and profitable in many different ways.

3. Successful business people are cold-hearted and insensitive.

Oh... my favorite lie about business! Business practices have become cold-hearted and insensitive, that is true. But people, especially successful people, are actually loving and caring. We have just shifted our vision of success to having a lot of money. Honestly, people who do great in business, live comfortably but will not do it by having their employees and clients pay for it.

If you're cold-hearted that means you're not passionate. And...

...if you're not passionate about what you're doing every day, you won't be as successful as you can be.

Your mind just wouldn't be as inspired and productive. Your body will become sick and tired. People around you will not be inspired either, so they won't be as productive and inspired either! Efficiency requires things to be done in the best way possible. Lack of sensitivity doesn't allow you to be the best. It also doesn't allow you to acknowledge the importance of human and natural resources. In the long-run pollution, discrimination, and all those negative practices, become expensive.

4. The #1 focus of a successful business is profit.

Profit is important for survival, and definitely a key performance indicator. But if you focus on growing your profits, you lose track of why your business exists. Your business has a purpose, values, mission, vision, etc. Whether you wrote them out and promote them or you just have them in your mind. They are your reason for being. Therefore, they permeate all through your business practices.

Your focus, if you want a truly successful business practice, should be the value you bring to yourself and others.

If you focus on that, you'll sell more, produce in a better and more ethical way, and have a long-running business. We overestimate the value of money and underestimate the value of living in peace. A good night of sleep, quality time with our loved ones, a healthy body, and good relationship with others and the planet.

5. The customer is always right.

One more way we tried to use catchy phrases to make things easier, while making a mess. If the customer is always right, then everyone else would have to be wrong all the time, right? That, in itself, is a recipe for disaster. If the business or staff are all wrong, then how can you sell? If the company isn't doing the right things. How can it innovate?

> ***Businesses are relationships. They are thus, based on the value we bring to each other.***

As a business developer, owner, or just employee, you need to know that. What are you bringing to the relationship? Not just with your customer, but with your teammates? How about your company? Providers? Community?

You have to know what's best for your customer, by getting to know both, your product and service, as well as your customer's needs. Most of the time your customer will come in looking for something because of their personal experience. If you know your business, you will be able to find whatever suits them best, while keeping their highest good in mind, and the best way in which YOU can provide value to them. They are not mutually exclusive!

If you care for all of them, and pay attention to what they say:

a) You grow and learn.
b) You find areas of growth and opportunity.
c) You learn from your mistakes.
d) You increase and highlight your value.
e) And... You can build long-lasting relationships based on trust. Your customer will know and trust that you will always do what brings them the most value!

Beyond the lies about business and money.

I have noticed that every time I fall for the lies about business and money... My business struggles, and I struggle with it.

When I stay true to my purpose, my values, and the trust-based relationship with my clients, my business grows.

And what does business growth mean? I have bigger and better projects, that align with my purpose and goals, more income, and I can provide better opportunities for other professionals to collaborate. It means, I have a business that fits my life, I don't "work for a living".

3. Why and How Matter the Most.

When you look inside
Into your heart of hearts
What makes it beat?
What brings joy and light?
Let that spark shine bright
And light your path
For one step, then two, or maybe a mile.
You never know whose walk
May come to life
By the light you shine
Or the path you start.

The more I learn about people's live stories, the more I validate that our intention is the most important ingredient in our actions. Many profitable businesses give millions away in charities, while their actual business practices are harming more than they can heal. They are giving back, just to get tax cuts, or get better public perception. It may be good for business, but is it good for them as human beings? Good for the world? Good for the people who work with and for them?

Why and how matter the most. Even if we would like to think our actions matter more than our motivation. It may seem like a series of shortcuts to ease our conscience, but we know better.

In my business practice, very often, clients come to me saying "I don't know what to do". But I have learned in time, that WHAT may be the easiest answer. Interestingly, what really flows naturally when you get clear on your values, your motivation, and your purpose. That's why, regardless of the service I'm providing my clients, the first thing I ask them and help them figure out is WHY AND HOW they want to operate.

Why and how matter the most!

Every single time. I know this. Every single time I go around that reasoning, things don't work out. When I offer my assistance, or join a project where my client doesn't have a clear why and how, the potential for chaos is unleashed. Results don't come, and frustration becomes a constant. This happens because, believe it or not, we are more emotional and purpose-based than we want to admit.

We tend to enjoy saying we are rational beings, trying to change our thoughts and our ideas. But the truth is, our emotions and motivation are a key element to our daily routines, our communication, interactions, and basically, to our every decision and action.

Our "why", our motivation, will redirect all of the shortcomings that our ideas may have. We may question our skills, our resources, and overall choices. But if there's a strong motivation for us to do it, we will always find a way to make things happen. If we do not know why we do things, half-way through our process, we will just quit. Hardships, accidents, crisis, and any other hurdle along the way, will make us take a different direction. But that won't happen if we are clear on our motivation.

Our intention and purpose, also filter into "how" we do things. I don't mean figuring out the technical "how". You can figure out a million ways to get to an outcome. The interesting questions to ask regarding your "how" are:

- Are you taking shortcuts?
- Are you avoiding conflict?
- Are you using people or working with them?
- Are you respectful of laws and regulations?
- Are you mindful of traditions and local practices?
- Are you respecting your values?
- Are you following universal values like: respect, freedom, dignity?
- Are you basing your choices on fear?
- Are you bringing your whole self?

Why you do what you do.
Your dreams and inspiration are a key part of who you are.

You may not give them credit regularly, but they will come back to haunt you if you hide them in the closet.

If you grew up wishing you could be an astronaut, a singer, or a race car driver, it matters! You may decide not to pursue that specific career path. Life, needs, or choices may have led you away. As I have mentioned before, your dreams may not come true exactly the way you envisioned them. A version of that passion project may become your daily reality, but there was something deep within you, making it show up.

You need to remember why those dreams were part of you. It's worth to take a look at your past. Maybe you wanted to be a ballerina because you liked music, movement, beauty. It didn't necessarily mean you wanted to be a ballerina, but you liked what it represented. Why?

Maybe you wanted to become a doctor, and you ended up studying law. Did that lead you away from your dream? Be honest with yourself, and dig deep. You could have always wanted to help others, and make things better for them. Both occupations can do that, you can still honor the essence of your dream, and be practical or change your mind. Circumstances and life events change our paths all the time.

The most important thing is to be true to who we know ourselves to be.

Your purpose, whether you believe in a divine calling, or a practical reason for your existence, exists. You see where you fit. You see what you bring to society. Your gifts and skills are put in alignment with something else. It really doesn't matter if it's the supply chain, the organization's mission, or your inner calling. There is a WHY to your being here and now. Whatever it is you're doing, there is a why.

How do you do it?
I'm a sucker for biopics and documentaries. I have to admit it, learning more about the life path and journey that people take is one of my passions. Our personal evolution is a testament to our identity, our environment and our loyalty to the potential within us.

I have seen people turned into heroes and benchmarks of success merely because they made a lot of money. Regardless of the path of damage and misery that they left along the way. I have seen people called "respectable" even after stepping over each and every one of the people around them. They achieved their "vision", yes but at what cost to the collective? Being "the first" who did something is valued. But rarely do we mention those who fixed all the chaos that "the first" ones left behind.

For example, many music producers have been deemed as the "makers" of an artist's career. I myself have worked with singers, producers, music labels, etc. I know the constant struggle between the creators and the marketers. The business side, and the inspiration side, and the delicate balance around them.

I know some singers were created as mere products. They were told what do sing, what to do, say, and promote. Some were lucky enough to have their "characters" loosely based on their personalities. Most, were not. When you see those twenty-something artists struggling with drugs, after huge success in their teenage years. That's usually why.

Was it worth it? People who have lost their identity, their self-worth, and in some cases, their health or their life for the sake of what? Fame? Fortune? Who benefited from that? Do they enjoy it?

I have seen singer come off a stage after being praised by thousands of people singing their songs, only to get on a van and cry, drink, or escape their loneliness in whatever way they can. I have seen people find their identity in becoming the "right hand" of an artist, because they couldn't figure out who they were on their own. And, I have seen wonderful success stories of artists with a happy and healthy family life, great performances, successful records, and truly loved within the industry.

What's the difference between all of them? Their "why"? Not really, it's mostly HOW. The things they agreed to. They things they were or weren't willing to compromise or sacrifice for the sake of "making it". The boundaries they set. The dignity they gave themselves and others.

It's the music producer who understands the essence of the artist, protects it, and promotes it. It's the artist who understands the hard work that the team has put together, from the people who set-up the stage, the media, marketers, managers, musicians, and audience. Those who know that "how" you do things, matters.

I'll go deeper into this in the following chapters, but first I want to throw a quick…

LOVE CHALLENGE ALERT!

Before you launch your next product or campaign ask yourself:
Is this good to me? To society? The planet? How about the community? Am I doing this the cleanest, fairest, most loving and honest way I can?

A deep and honest "why": Because of love.

Going back to the biopics and documentaries. How many times have you seen, heard or read that someone did "it" because of love? Because they loved cars, the environment, their country, others... Because they loved drawing, or singing, or basketball... Check it out.

How many business people became business owners and built their business around a product or service they loved? Not just because the market demanded it. Or perhaps because they "could" or had the resources to do it. How many leaders and public figures devoted their lives to their passion?

It may sound too romantic, idealistic or naïve. But I can bet you, the people who ran companies successfully without ever complaining of how long it took them to build them, or what they sacrificed, did so out of love. True passion and commitment with what they did.

Many have accomplished the unimaginable because of a big event that made an impact in their lives. A disease, a death, loss, struggle, war... You name it, there was a trigger that unleashed an intense passion and love for making things happen.

That's where obstacles, struggle, complications, competition, crisis, and all of those things take the back seat. Your mission through passion, will come first in a constructive way. Not in the "tragic artist" or workaholic-Scrooge kind of way. Not in the "end justifies the means" kind of way. It's the positive "getting through it all", and "enjoying the ride" and "this little light of mine" kind of way.

There's an economic acronym that I learned while studying Business and Economics in college:

IIWI: Is it worth it?

I learned to use it not just for economic, investment, or consumer-choices. It became the question to ask for every activity, relationship, project, and choice. The secret here, is that when you operate from love... When you choose doing what you love, for your loved ones, out of love for yourself and others... The answer will always be: YES!

Doing good.

When I was growing up, I remember thinking that anyone who was really successful had most likely done it at the expense of others. I used to think that you had to give up something in order to succeed. You probably had to give up having friends, free-time, or even principles and morals. That's what I saw around me. Working hard and being successful seemed to be all of that.

Let me share with you a very personal story. My dad used to work for a cigarette company. He was very proud, because he was doing very well in the company. He could provide for us, private schools, trips, etc. I, on the other hand, was miserable. To me, he worked for a company that made the product that made my grandmother smoke all day long, and thus made me sneeze, cough and have "colds" all the time.

A couple of years went by, and commercials about "smoking may cause cancer" came up. Now my disturbance with his occupation was bigger. It wasn't just that I was getting sick from second-hand smoke. I actually asked him, straight forward: "How can you work for a company that kills people?"

That specific view of what he did for a living, shaped me for good. I was committed to doing things differently. I may have been 7 years-old, but I had a certainty. I could not be part of a business, company, or organization who was hurting others. At least, not if I was aware of it.

My dad's experience was not an exception. It was usually the rule for everyone around me. Friends and family would share their stories in parties and reunions. They were working for this corrupt company that had to bribe the officials to get their product imported. They had a boss that had them skip a step of the process because he didn't have the time to wait for things to come through. The project that the company wouldn't get because they wouldn't go out for drinks, golfing, or even to a strip club with the Marketing guy who was in charge of the account. All of those were really off-putting stories.

When I got into High School, my school's motto was "to become, in order to serve". The moment I saw it for the first time, it all just clicked with me. All the wisdom, all the success, and all the things that I could gain had a purpose. A purpose that connected me with more than my ego, my needs, and my vision. The question was... Was this just another "nice quote" that everyone uses, but no one lives by? Could it really happen?

It wasn't until my college years that I was finally proved right. As I studied business, and success stories about companies worldwide, I learned that there was another way to do business. An ethical, values-based, people-first way. And guess what... it was profitable! It wasn't easy, but over the years, as I followed the companies I had studied, I noticed they did great!

It doesn't matter if you're running a multi-million-dollar corporation worldwide, or an online business from your living room.

You can do GOOD for yourself and others.

This means that if you preach that family comes first, you indeed make time for family. But here comes the game-changer. This is not just for yourself. You do it for everyone that does business with you! Your employees, customers, and community know that you live and breathe by this value, and you will share it with them.

When you advertise that you are guided by a set of values or principles, then you build your business practices around them. Anywhere from caring for the planet to providing free education resources for underprivileged families. It is not just about donating to charity. That's the simple tax-deductible solution. But the easier and more rewarding path is to build-in your values to every single practice. Instead of donating to charity, how about scholarships for the families of your employees? Instead of just planting trees, how about making sure you use procedures and products that are cleaner and better for the environment? Include plants and maybe even orchards or crops within your office-space so people can eat healthier and more natural meals?

Nowadays it's even more noticeable. You'll see a full-range of companies that are operating from their values and making things work for their employees. They may not be perfect, and still have ways to improve, but they're doing it.

From healthy office-spaces with baby-sitting resources or pet-friendly environments, to local sourcing or organic ingredients.

You can do good.

Stop listening to the noise.

A couple of years in the "real world" brought me back to my usual programming, after the bubble of love and positivity that I experienced in college. There is so much noise out there! When you're young, trying to prove yourself, and face the "real" world, there are many lessons to learn.

Interesting fact, most of the noise comes from our own minds! The obsession with being rational ruins the most basic of our principles. We devote so much time and attention to "learning", and getting more knowledge into our minds. And, by all means, I fully support learning, and gaining knowledge. But...

No amount of knowledge will ever compensate what your purpose, motivation, and values can do for you!

Why and how matter most, because they open doors that no amount of resources and connections can surpass. I have been involved in projects with millions of dollars invested, teams with skillful and qualified people, that amount to very little long-term impact.

But then, there comes a little project with little resources, and one or two people who lay their lives on the line, and change everything around them. One or two people who listened to their passion, their purpose and to the values that they had within. And you can see it! You can see how they inspire everyone they touch. Anyone and everyone who interacts with them grows. Regardless of the trends, the industry, the political situation, or the algorithm.

When you get clear on why you do what you do, and how you are going to do it, what you do flows naturally.

That doesn't mean that clarity will come easy, or fast. You may need to fall and fail a couple of times. But, trust me, every lesson learned will be worth it!

Saying no.

Living your life, while sticking to your purpose and your values may require you to say "no" to things that seemed like the obvious choice. There may be tempting opportunities that appear to be easy, fast, simple, and profitable. But if you do them in spite of having every cell in your body cry "no!", they will not feel as good as they seemed.

That's the really loud noise. The fear, trauma, and pain of others, and even your own past crawling back to you. All of these things may reason their way to your mind, but you do know better!

We are also creatures of habit. Many of the choices that you may think come rationally, actually just come out of habit. "That's the way it has always been done." It's more than just a phrase, it's a set of collective patterns! And it's not that simple or easy to detach yourself from them.

We are also social animals. We go with the flow. We want to fit in, even though when we talk about business and marketing, we may always talk about how you want to "stand out". As part of a collective society, egotistic and individualistic as it may be, we find safety in community.

As we move forward, I will also make a point of how essential it is for you to find your pack, or team, or support system. But, we cannot just go with the flow if and when we notice that we are walking straight into the void. We cannot follow the community or the collective when it's heading directly into the destruction of our planet, lack of universal values, disrespect for some kind of harmony and well-being. At that point in time, it is worth it to swim upstream, or stop and let the crowd go by.

When you struggle with all the things you have to say "no" to, it's best to think about the things you are welcoming into your life by saying no. If you say "no" to that project that was quick and easy income, you're saying "yes" to valuable and good projects. You may be saying no to a steady income, but then again, you may be saying yes to honesty, fairness, equality, non-discrimination, human rights, etc.

Boundaries are helpful in any relationship. And businesses are relationships. Saying "no" to things that don't align with your why and how, is your way to set a clear and loving boundary with the business world and economic system, not to mention society as a whole.

What happens when why and how align?
When why and how align, everything flows!

I probably would not believe how real this is if it hadn't happened to me. But when you are in alignment, you find connections, collaborations and resources that unblock everything that reason, connections, effort, and technology couldn't unblock.

When you own your purpose and values, you make better choices. And even when situations and scenarios may change, you will be more able to react. That is why, even when you may be in survival mode, striving to find the next paycheck or pay that loan, if you are in alignment, you will find more options and opportunities to meet those needs. When you are not aligned, you may only see the more obvious and sometimes burdensome solutions. Hey... They may even be illegal. Temptation will come your way, and you will always have a choice.

Why and how matter the most! It feels like magic, but it's just coherence. Being all of who you really are. Your ideas, your skills, your values, and dreams. They all come together to allow you to step fully into YOU. Balance, prosperity, success... the description is irrelevant. It just feels good! You do great, and it feels good!

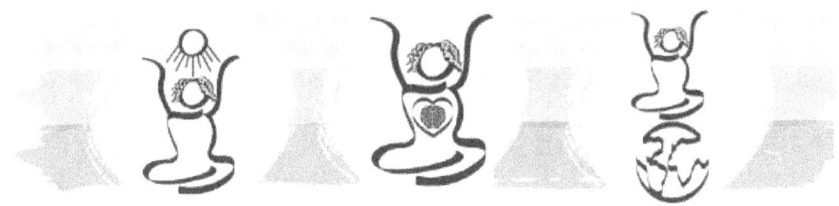

4. Welcome to The Love Economy

Love is the air I breathe.

Love is the work my body does with it.

Love is me moving, thinking, praying…

Love is the money I make.

Love is the stand I take.

My thoughts and actions show love.

My heartbeat and my money show love.

Every action, every thought, every moment

Love…

Every "thank you", "I'm here", "I'm with you"…

Love…

Every YES and every NO

Love…

Every color, every face, friend or foe

Love…

Welcome to the love economy! I know, how can we talk about love when the whole planet is in chaos, right?

You know how everyone is fighting over the damage of capitalism? The dangers of socialism? The epic fail of communism?

Most of what's going on with these conversations, happens because we keep trying to make old models work in a new economy. We have gone beyond globalization and neoliberalism to a new model. The love economy!

It's time for a shift in perception.

It's not the system that has failed. As I just mentioned, we keep trying to make new models fall into old paradigms. Our shift is actually catching up with the reality surrounding us. The shift in perception is also being forced by the social, political, and environmental crisis. All voices keep pointing in the same direction, no matter how much we try to avoid it.

Regardless of personal bias, love is bigger and undeniable. This is why things are shifting. The little pieces of wisdom that we are all bringing into the system, are providing more clarity for society as a whole. Not only is it unbearable to endure injustice and racism, it is actually unsustainable.

A new economy, the love economy.

What are the basics of this new system? Simple:

- *people matter*
- *the environment is a priority*
- *growth must be sustainable*

What does this mean?

People matter.

It means that the humanity of people as they perform any activity is important. We are talking about dignity, fulfillment, and fair wages for employees. We are admitting that happy people are productive, healthy, and a better investment. People want products and services that match their values and needs.

Acting in any other way, making anything else a priority, will not do. Whatever you build, produce, or sell needs someone to buy it, use it, or consume it. Taking people out of the equation seems nonsensical.

CRITICAL QUESTION:

Then, why have we been doing it?

The environment is a priority.

We can no longer make this a side goal. Humanity cannot keep creating products that we cannot dispose of properly. We are no longer willing to put growth above sustainability. We know better.

Creative solutions and innovation have shown us we can do things better. And if we don't, there is always someone on the other side of the world who might. It does not matter how wealthy you are, you will breathe the same air, and eat the same toxins as the rest of the world.

The environment is a priority, because, we haven't found another planet where we could live. And even if we did so, we need to learn how to keep this one, if we want to find the keys to make any other planet habitable.

Growth must be sustainable.

The old mindset of "I win- you lose" is over. We have seen the unsustainable warfare and violence worldwide. That is not an accident. It is entirely our doing.

That crazy idea of making a profit out of others, without any foreseeable consequence, is gone. It's simply bad business and wasteful allocation of resources to exploit our resources. It does not matter how much money you are willing to spend on defense, protection, bribes, sanctions, fees, and other similar concepts.

We have a health crisis, because we chose to make medicine a business, as opposed to understanding that health is an asset. We have a humanitarian crisis, because we chose to make war a business, as opposed to understanding peace as an asset.

The best way to do things is in a way that you don't have to spend more resources making up for your mistakes.

This means that, whatever you do, it has to be done in a way that you do not harm others. By doing so, you create a chain of positive impact. Such a chain will allow you to focus on doing what you do and love, better, faster, cheaper, and with less complications.

That's just wishful thinking!

Thinking about a love economy is not wishful thinking. On the contrary! Take a look at the world's success stories.

Would you have imagined that one of the world's most successful businesses is a free platform that connects people? Would you have imagined you would pay to stay at a stranger's house when you visited another country? What products and services make Oprah Winfrey one of the wealthiest and most influential people in the planet?

Ever heard of Corporate Social Responsibility? CSR is an actual measure of success and recognition to good business practices. It encompasses all the practices put in place by companies in order to uphold the principles of sustainable development.

There is also ESG (Environmental Social and Governance) that refers to the three key factors when measuring the sustainability and ethical impact of an investment in a business or company.

The love economy connects entrepreneurs worldwide!

That is an additional element of this new age. People have little to no desire to be employed. Chains, collectives, and groups of entrepreneurs are creating new business dynamics.

People doing what they love most, and selling it to those who want it. They do not need the pension plan and benefits. No need for corporate offices. They are turning their passion projects into successful businesses.

As if that was not enough, people do not devote their whole life to one career. We are living longer lives, in different ways. We are now free to learn, grow, and collaborate outside of an office environment, while making a living. More productive systems are being developed. Systems where your knowledge, skills and passions are valued. And at the core of all of them, is the love for our-selves, our families, and the lifestyle we decide to create for ourselves.

Are you ready for the love economy? Because it's here, just waiting for you!

41

5. There IS crying in business.

Stop fighting emotion

What does that tear want to tell you?

What does that pang in your stomach mean?

What is that smile showing you?

Listen to it.

That tear, that pang, that smile…

They are all reminders of your humanity, your story, and your connection to others.

Listen to them.

From the first time I watched the movie "A League of Their Own" I couldn't let go of that line. "There's no crying in baseball! That moment when Tom Hanks's character made it very clear that the coach mistreats the players, because that's the way the game is. One of the female players, instead of "taking it like a man", cries. The rest of the team brings some comfort, but the coach doesn't change. Not right then at least.

So many misconceptions in one scene! Why are we supposed to justify rudeness and impoliteness with authority? Why would anyone, male or female, be treated that way? I am pretty sure that some world champions may have practiced "crying in baseball" when an injury left them out of that one key game. Or when they finally got to carry the trophy.

We've been fed that lie over and over in business. We have been shown that if a woman is to succeed in a "man's world" such as business, she has to be as cold, and ruthless, and insensitive. Supposedly learning from the qualities that make men successful in the business world. Well I think it is time to change that.

Even our top female leaders and thinkers, like Sheryl Sandberg and Joanna Barsh, have said that they had to adapt to the "male" way of behaving in business. I agree, it's hard, we need to keep fighting and change mindsets. But if our top leaders are preaching "adapting" to the wrong mindset as a key to success, then we haven't succeeded yet.

We need to have men engage in family raising and more social engagements. Women need to step up and admit their greatness without having to ask for permission or forgiveness in the process. Men and women learning to use their emotions as a building block, not as a power tool or destructive force. But… this war on emotions and glorification of "rationality" is a load of dirt piling under the rug of humanity and nurturing inhumanity.

We need more crying in business!
We need more men and women who are affected and transformed by what goes wrong in the world.

We need people who are ashamed and overwhelmed by the evil that surrounds them; but not so much as to be paralyzed by fear or crying in a corner. And for the record, that is not what women do.

Yes, we break, and we cry; but we get up, and we do whatever is needed to fix what is broken. We have brought up generation after generation of children—many times neglected by men who decided they had to be all about business.

The beauty of it, is that we now have new generations of men who refuse to buy that lie. And women, who refuse to carry along with it. We have men who want paternity leave and cherish holding their kids when they cry and won't say "stop crying", or "real men don't cry."

Now is the time for us to embrace the emotional side of business. Encouraging men and women who promote vulnerability as part of leadership. A leadership by example, showing that success comes from overcoming fear, and failure, and self-doubt, and attacks. As opposed to an apparent immunity to emotions.

Perhaps that's why biographical series and movies have become so influential in our times. That is why reality television became so big as well. We were finally shown that behind closed doors and curtains, success is messy. We began to learn that success was more than an uphill struggle. It really is a rollercoaster ride!

However, the cost of success reduces thoroughly when more and more humane people take control. You won't do "whatever it takes", because it won't be acceptable. You won't step over other people, because they will call you out as you do it. You will make mistakes, and you will continue to go down wrong roads, because that is what builds experience and character. Not as your "weak spots", but as your journey.

Given this, there is no need to throw people under the bus, or delight in their disgrace. There is no need for people around you to make mistakes more painful. Even though we may strive to please others, our deepest desires lie within ourselves. There is enough fear within us, of what we can or cannot achieve. Even without a destructive competitive survival-of-the-fittest environment, there is plenty to be learned within our own nature.

So, here is the little secret that not many business gurus will share with you.

You will cry, and after fighting and struggling you may get to the top, or not. The TOP doesn't matter anymore. It's about who you become not what you achieve.

That said, you will do great, only if you really took the time appreciate every step of the process. Enjoy the journey.

Not just crying… Emotions rule.

One of the most crucial elements for success when you focus on living from your soul are your emotions. Handling your feelings and emotions has become quite literally a life or death required skill. Depression, stress, anxiety, and frustration are the worst enemies of your personal success.

All of these things become almost unavoidable in today's world. We all rely so much on approval, success, results, income, and proving yourself to be useful.

As you're swimming upstream in a world that is still packed with people who think you're being naïve or childish by promoting a loving world. All this resistance can take a huge toil in your mental and emotional stability.

You are your biggest asset! Take care of yourself.

Most of what we are taught in school are technical skills. We become really good at communicating, calculating, memorizing, developing, and even creating. However, all of those skills and knowledge go down the drain when we spend hours stuck in traffic, had a fight with our mom, and cannot seem to pay the bills even after working ten hours a day.

Self-knowledge along with emotional intelligence make the difference. Knowing yourself, your history, what triggers, inspires and heals you. Handling your emotions, from the most beautiful excitement to the deepest and most painful sadness or anger. How does your body feel? Can you name more than ten emotions (there are way more)? What events trigger trauma from your childhood? What smells or sounds make you smile reminding you of a great moment?

These may all seem very casual questions, but they are not. When your emotions get the best of you, you need to know how to regain control. When pain and pressure put you down, you need to know what gets you back up. When others are feeling anxious or bullied, you need to know how to become an ally for them. We need to manage our emotions, and to manage our emotions as we interact with others.

Not enough

We live in a reality where marketers, society, and peer pressure keep telling you that you're not enough. You need to have this in order to be happy. You need to become, get or buy this to become worthy and accepted. You need to achieve this in order to succeed.

The economic concept of "scarcity" is what moves the economy, and it has taken control of our lives and mindsets. It basically means that someone wants or needs (Demand) what we have and can give (Supply). But this is not just one of those "evils" of Capitalism. We can find it in all areas of our lives. Many people don't think they are enough to be loved, to belong to a group or community, to be respected, to be safe…

You may wonder: but isn't that one of our basic human desires? Doesn't it trigger improvement and growth as well? It does. Not having wisdom can make you learn, grow, travel. Not winning that medal, could inspire you to train harder, do a better job, join a different team. But let's not fool ourselves, we all know we've gone too far.

I have been there. I have the "good girl" trauma. I was the perfect A's student (honestly in the Mexican system it was always about numbers I kept the 10's and 100's coming even 9.8 or 98 hurt). I was the daughter that stayed out of trouble to gain my parent's acceptance. I was the friend that went the extra mile with the gifts to "keep" people happy, to make sure I would live up to their expectations of me. Sadly, it becomes a fake expectation of yourself. A draining one. And it hurts. It does so much damage!

I was usually best friends with others struggling with their own expectations, even while staying away from the perfect scores. The girl or boy who lived up to the "trouble" reputation. The cute guy who stopped trying to be smart because being "cute" was what was expected and accepted of him. The jock who focused on sports, because it would be unmanly to show sensitivity or an artistic side. The girl who couldn't get away from being called a "slut" even after being single and quiet for years.

So, you see how, regardless of which end of the spectrum held your comfort zone, we all experienced some of this. None of those expectations and pressure helped any of us grow or thrive. They hurt us. They made us push too much, or give up and surrender to whatever the world set as our path.

When you switch things around your life changes. When you flip the equation to assume that you ARE enough, without doing, having, acquiring, or achieving anything. You are ALWAYS worthy of respect, safety, and basic dignity. If you believe it, you also defend it. You don't need laws, standards, or grades to enforce what you "should" do. Everything and anything you do will lead you to good things.

Your basic premise is: you are enough.
Now the second: be grateful for what you have.

You not only are enough, but you have enough. If you can breathe, move, think, eat, speak, and love freely you have more than half of the planet has right now. Yes, you could desire more. Yes, you can build more. But not because you need it to "be", but because you can. Wonder, magic, potential and good things are overflowing you in that state.

Why does gratitude equal to having enough? Because as you do the mental exercise to start feeling thankful for the things you DO have, you notice just how many of your basic needs are covered. It will also make you much more sensitive to the lack of them. Seeing people who cannot walk, breathe, sleep, speak, work, move, and love freely will feel unnatural to you. And it should. That IS a good trigger and inspiration for you to do better. Making sure that everything you do, warrantees the same dignity for others, that you seek for yourself.

By the way, this has also become a great rule for people who start their own business or have to work as freelancers. There are many people around the world trying to sell you courses, products, and formulas to "set-up" your business. The truth is, yet again, YOU ARE ENOUGH and YOU HAVE ENOUGH.

Don't try to start a business by renting the shop, hiring people, and then see if your product works. Do it backwards! Whatever you have or can do right now, do it. Then build upon it! You don't need to have a huge list to sell your first product. You don't have to gain 1,000 followers to sell your first art piece. Grow from what you have, that will give you peace of mind, and financial freedom. Something that puts perhaps the most pressure on our physical, spiritual, emotional, and mental health.

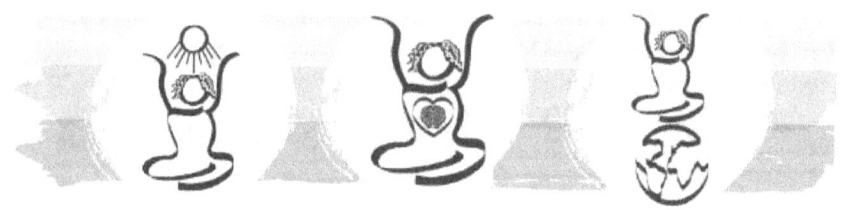

6. New Soul-filled Marketing

I hold a gift within me.
Even when I'm not ready to share it.
Even when people may not know they need it.
Sometimes it's taken years in the making.
Sometimes it just came to being.
I hold a gift within me.
I am grateful for my gift.
I am grateful that my gift is imperfect.
I am grateful for your gifts.
I am grateful that altogether they make the universe more loving, welcoming, and enjoyable.
I am grateful for our gifts and being able to give them.
They were meant to be shared, so I share mine in love, and hold yours in that same love.

Selling yourself doesn't mean selling your soul.

As a passionate marketer, I find it interesting to see that many people think branding is about creating a fake or make-believe identity.

Old-school marketing tried to make you fit into a set of guidelines to get to you to sell anything at any cost. But new-school marketing, has been mostly triggered by social media, and thus digital marketing, is very different.

Thank you, millennials, for proving that your true story and message sells!

Most old-school marketers will try to sell you magic solutions, "email templates" that will sell anything. Set structures that work "every time". Beware! That is not how true marketing works!

Not to say that there is nothing to learn from those formulas, techniques, and strategies. Not all sales and marketing courses or techniques are obsolete. However, there is no one strategy that works "every time" for "any" product or service.

Except, perhaps, marketing with truth.

Using these generic trends and templates is what makes you feel "empty" or like your selling your soul for the sake of making your business work. Conforming yourself to set stages, patterns, and containers drains your essence. As I've said before, we are all unique and different. What works for you may not work for me. Furthermore, what works right now, may not work… later today!

Constant change makes it difficult to stick to a plan or formula, even if you want to. Even if you developed the formula! And this is a great thing. You may not feel safe or comfortable because of it, but we are all much more adaptive, rich, and valuable because of it.

What you really need to make your business work is PROMOTING YOUR SOUL; sharing with others why your business, content or service makes your soul feel good.

The beauty of social media, and true content marketing, is the opportunity to share stories, experiences, and knowledge. It is to provide content that brings value to users. Social media was built to connect, and tell stories! So, if you really want to find the best way to sell, you need to get two things straight:

Your message

Your message includes your story, who you are and what you're doing.

- What sort of product, service, or content you'll be sharing.
- Why is this important to you?
- Why do you think it should be important to others?

This will give you clarity on how you fit with the rest of the economy.

Your values

Your values are part of who you are.

- What do you stand for?
- Where did your message come from?
- What makes your message true and valuable?

This will help you attract the right crowd to your message.

True marketing doesn't sell everything to everyone. It just helps both sides of the economic transaction be found, connect, and understand whether they meet each other's needs and expectations.

This is why true, honest, and soulful marketing works best! And this is why you will be appealing to the right audience if you get your message and values right. The next step is the strategy, the channels, and those cool things that you can actually learn from those marketing specialists who are trying to reach out to you.

Utilitarian businesses and economic models talk about "what you get" out of a business transaction. We are way beyond that! We are living in a relationship-based era. You are building a relationship with everyone around you. That includes your clients! It goes beyond cost-benefit.

Toxic marketing even goes further. It is based on the fact that you have to persuade the other that they "need" you. Remember, our sense of lack? You are not going to be happy until you wear this shirt, drink this juice, buy these glasses, and attend this event. Your business will not succeed unless you hire me, buy this, use that. No need for any of that, not anymore.

Soulful marketing helps you build a relationship. That's why it becomes so crucial to build it in honesty. It doesn't need to be complicated or elaborate. Who are you and what do you bring to this relationship? And who are you looking for?

In an era where many people strive for millions of likes and followers, the best kept secret is that loyal followings come from treating each one of your followers like the one most important person in your business, brand, and environment. And it doesn't work if it's not authentic.

Quick marketing tip:
Keep it short, sweet, real and soulful!

Understand Why You're Afraid of Branding Yourself

One of the big struggles that I've found with customers and friends while developing their own branding is a certain fear of putting your face and name out there.

I can absolutely relate! As a producer, manager, and consultant I have spent most of my life building someone else's brand, name, and popularity. I find it very comfortable to see all the pieces, put them together, and walk hand in hand with my friends and clients to share their gifts with the world. But when it comes to working your own brand, it may not come so easy.

I have been confident and comfortable knowing how to set up my client's essence in anything from business cards to massive shows. But when to myself, it requires a personal process. Sometimes it's enlightening. Sometimes, it becomes painful. Looking at our own story may be a wonderful journey, but life has a way to unearth wounds and trauma when you least expect it.

A new job opportunity, position, or project may come bearing gifts. However, some of those gifts, may only be revealed after you've dealt with a few demons. Perhaps, that is why so many of us are reluctant to change. We may know what to expect, even if it is not what we want or desire.

That comfort, however, is an illusion. Nothing stays constant. It has never been that way. Anyone who cherishes the "good old days" has chosen to forget or neglected to see the pain and mistakes of the past. While there is always something to learn in our history, we are exactly where we need to be in the here and now. Acknowledging our here and now, allows us to see more opportunities, and enjoy our growth.

Be present, be mindful.

Using your name as your brand makes you visible.

When you tell someone that their name is their brand, many people become intimidated.

Some people find that using their name as their brand, puts them at the center of a stage. There is nowhere to hide. You are out there, no cover, no façade, no shelter.

To some it may pose the challenge of keeping the vanity in our egos in check. To others, it challenges them to embrace all of who they are. The light and the shadow. Because we are all a little bit of both.

How is it that I won't get dizzy with power and fame? And on the other hand, am I running away from "fame" because of personal insecurities?

Some people need a character or a brand name to make things work. Some artists go with a pseudonym or artistic name, and it works for them. Some business owners may create a brand. It helps keep their personal life separate from the private.

However, in both cases, your essence will be on display. It may be more evident when you use your own personal or family name. But even when you create a character, there is enough of you in it, even if you try to hide your true self.

Whichever may be the case, you want to make sure that your brand is trusted. And, the best asset to be trusted is to put yourself out there. Yes, that means your name, your face, and who you are in the most truthful way.

You may find that as you use your name and face to grow a brand, you also have to deal with plenty of insecurities. It is a process, a very delicate process that will make you face things about yourself that you might have putting away for years.

In the past it was mostly public figures who faced this process. Did you ever notice some beautiful artists who destroyed their bodies and faces with surgeries? Looking at themselves so much created a distorted perception of themselves. This happens to you and me nowadays with social media. Even more, when you choose to become the face of your brand.

Be honest... How many times do you check how you look in a video call? How many times do you check to see if that photo of yourself got enough likes and comments?

Do I have authority over what I'm saying?

Why do people want to learn from or about me?

It's not unusual to have those doubts and insecurities. It's now commonly known as "impostor syndrome". But those doubts don't have to be a bad thing necessarily. As a matter of fact, your sales pitch and your branding efforts will most of the time be derived from such questions.

Each of those questions are actually part of YOUR marketing pitch if you can take the time to answer them. You're capable, instructed, or experienced enough to share your voice and your talent. Every time you come up with why you're "good enough" write it down, that will make good and honesty copy to help you promote your product or service.

The reasons why you're selling something or doing something are exactly what makes you "good enough" to do or sell it.

Next time you feel afraid of branding yourself... Just remember that the first argument in favor of why you're doing anything is the actual courage that it takes for you to do it. Whoever has enough bravery to put themselves out there and share what they know, think, believe, or can do is worth listening to.

After that, it takes connection, quality of message, delivery, format, and plenty of other things for your message to spread and connect. But the first step and measure of validity for you to be "out there" is definitely to have the courage to be "out there".

Selling Yourself vs. Selling Your Service

Is it the same thing?

As a branding professional I know that your story, your values, and your strengths make your brand. I know that may sound like a very simplistic view, but it is true. In a way all those things make your business persona, thus selling your SELF. Your strengths are directly related to what you do for your clients.

You may be a marketing professional, business consultant, productivity expert, motivational coach, fitness expert, nutritionist, etc. Whatever your occupation, your strengths should be in there if you are working on your own. You are your own brand, your CEO, and your marketing team, all in one. We know this, but do you also want to be the face of your brand or not really?

Many business strategies, and online marketing experts, base their strategy in your brand. Many of their strategies turn you into an influencer. This is something that I have promoted as well. Many of my clients are set and ready to become influencers and experts, thus promoting themselves as their brands. However, not everyone is built to be an influencer and superstar. Some people thrive by working backstage. They love team work, and helping build other people's businesses and brands. And that is not a bad thing!

Personal branding, and business branding is not a one-size-fits-all strategy. Therefore, not everyone is going to be a top-shelf influencer. Even though we are ALL influencers to our immediate communities.

What we now see as influencers, are really celebrities. Those people who actually use their names and platforms to sell. Not only their own products, and services, but others as well.

What happens if you want to build trust and sell your services but not your SELF

If you are trying to provide more service and build your brand through reputation, more than influence or media presence, your plan is different. The strategy that will work best will be the following:

1. Be clear about what you offer.
2. Build a reputation through satisfied clients.
3. Grow your clients encouraging referrals (through discounts, bonuses, or preferred plans).
4. Highlight customer experience, stories, and testimonials.
5. Share success stories. (respecting confidentiality and specific names and details.)

These are pretty broad and general guidelines. The specifics of content and digital strategy depend on your style and values. As well as the platforms that your clients may prefer. Again, there is no quick fix or template that works for everyone.

These are just tips for you to understand that not all trends focus on Facebook lives and growing numbers or lists. Some strategies can be focused on value, and quality of your experiences and services.

Stop selling lies and giving marketing a bad name.

Many modern marketers use and recommend using false promising results. They are selling lies for all practical purposes. Miracle statements like "become a millionaire" or "lose # pounds in # weeks" may trigger the best gut responses and easy sales pitches.

> *However, marketing, when done right, is an art. Honest and soulful.*

Here are three basic elements of good and high-quality soulful marketing:

1. **Good storytelling**
2. **Added value**
3. **Catering to your client's needs**

Good Storytelling

Infomercials and reality shows are the best proof. Knowing the story of your product, or the stories of those who use it, works wonders! It appeals to basic psychology and social impulse, in a positive way. You may still sell aspirational concepts, and show before and after. But you do so in a way that allows your user to connect with the product or service.

When you learn that Apple and Amazon started in someone's garage, you are not beings sold a lie. It is aspirational. When you learn that Walt Disney was broke and ended up building an empire, it is true. Hard work pays off. And your connection with their stories may encourage you to build your own success story.

Sharing your inspiration with others, allows them to develop empathy for your product or service. And this, may be compelling to their decision to buy.

Added Value

True marketing is like match-making. You want the right people to find the right product (or service). Storytelling is one way to do it, but it is incomplete if you do not tell your audience what they get out this business transaction. If they buy your product, then they will what? They will have more time, save money, learn more, be happier, healthier, more relaxed, etc. You know it! Fill in the blank! And if you don't know yet, try your best to figure it out soon.

Provide them with the result, but also give them value. This is one of the things that people struggle with when they start working in a new mindset. We are conditioned to ask: "What's in it for me?" Particularly when you've been wronged, cheated or exploited. But our new mindset isn't just about direct benefit. It also has an added value!

When you buy this product, you are supporting this cause. By joining my list, you will receive these benefits. Or just saying: "Every time you purchase one of my products, you are supporting a small family-owned business that employs local talent." Just be real. No lies needed! Your product or service, not only serves a specific purpose, it is also part of a bigger cause.

Catering to Your Client's Needs

Know your client. This means, knowing where they are, what they need, what they do, and how and where you fit in. Nothing is better in this business-client relationship than feeling important. And what makes us feel important? To know that someone cares about who we are and what we think.

If you listen to your client, and analyze their behavior, you are better able to serve. It's the good old "market research". Millions have been spent by advertisers and corporations trying to get to know their users. Now, there's social media, and your overall customer experience. You can get to know your user simply by opening a channel where they can communicate with you, and you with them. Sounds familiar? (Hint: It can be as elaborate as an app, or as simple as immediate feedback in a conversation as you close your sale.)

This goes beyond stalking or invading privacy. Pixels and other tracking tools may be helpful, but they are not essential. I'm talking about learning from what your client already shows you. That is if you're paying attention.

You do not need sneaky tricks, all you need is to take the time, or find the right people to stay informed. Talk to your users. You can hire a market research company or person, for sure! But you can also do it on your own. If you have a team, you can also show them how to engage with users.

Whichever tool or resource you choose to use, the real key concept is to take your clients seriously. Each one of them is a person. They have a story, and something to teach you about your brand and their relationship with it.

Even if every specific choice and trait can create patterns, each client is different. Never forget that! If you learn to cherish this when you have just one customer in front of you, you will most likely remember it when you have to keep track of them with serial numbers or client ID's.

At this point, I need to remind you of something important. Every time I talk about clients and customers, you could very easily switch the word to "partner", "supplier", etc. Remember that the new business mindset sees everyone who engages with your business as a relationship. So, whatever applies to the relevance of your client, will apply to your suppliers as well. Whatever applies to your well-being, will apply to that of your employees, clients, associates, and community. Whatever applies to how you treat your customers and suppliers, also applies to how you run your relationship to yourself and your community.

It's a business ecosystem if that helps you keep track of things.

The value you cater to your client's needs includes their experience with your product, or brand. And that includes the product or service itself, but also the language and stories that you use to communicate with them. Respect them, and respect yourself. You are accountable for what you say.

This is precisely why I want to wrap up this chapter with a quote from Iliza Shlesinger, a stand-up comedian. Your perspective and what you're building with your actions and your values is the most important element to consider. Not because you're the most important person in the world. But because you are going to live with the consequences of your choices, your actions and your message!

> *The longer you go on, (...), the more you're going to have to contend with the things you've said, and do you really believe those. And sometimes we make mistakes in what we say, sometimes there will be things you wish you could take back. But by and large what are you saying? What are you building? What's your point of view.*

"Iliza Shlesinger: Hurts to Be Awesome. Chronic Pain, Comedy & the Mind-Body Connection", Mayim Bialik's Breakdown Podcast, Jan 26,2021.

7. Collaboration is not an option, it is a key to survival.

Each of us holds a piece.

A piece of wisdom that carries our story, our pain, and tears.

A piece of joy that carries our love, our passion and dreams.

Put them together.

We are all stronger, wiser, better.

Why do we insist on competing? Collaboration has proved once and again that it is the best key to success and business survival nowadays.

Old school marketing, and really all of business practices, are traditionally represented by the 80s and 90s Pepsi vs. Coke campaigns. The old mindset is the dirtiest kind of political campaign and dog-eat-dog business practice. The goal is to make sure everybody knows that my product is the best product ever. Most usually, making sure people know just how bad the "other guy" is. Practices go as far as making everything possible so that you're the last business standing, keeping all of the profits and market monopoly.

The new business mindset, and new marketing is totally different. While we will try to promote and boost the benefits of buying our product or service, we do not disregard others. We are not trying to take over all of the market, or the world for that matter.

In the new business mindset, if you win, we all win! Even if you're my competition. I can keep an eye on your practices and learn from your experience. We can develop technology that will reduce our joint costs, or create awareness about common areas of interest.

The use of social media has made this type of marketing bloom and thrive. Mainly, because seeing the social media environment as a whole, you can witness the most obvious and active global community.

This means that if you choose to see every participant as "competition", you'd be competing against singers, TV shows, sport teams, and any content creator in the whole globe. Really? Do you want to go there? I'll show you how this is the wrong approach as you continue to read this chapter…

We expanded the universe of consumers so much, that there is room for everyone to sell.

Our universe of consumers, or market, is now global. Why should we fight other consultants, artists, or products when we can never take care of a whole market? Even the biggest corporation in the world cannot provide the whole world of products. That certainly changes schemes, strategies, and obviously marketing.

In all honesty, ever since trade started, we understood that we needed each other. Civilizations were not ready to engage with each other and grow with each other. Our "survival of the fittest" mindset led to colonialism and exploitation. However, the root of it all was that no matter how big and powerful your empire was, you needed something from the others. Human resources, natural resources, technology, whatever the item may be, no one person, company, or country has it all.

These same terms apply to your business. From solopreneurs working from home to transnational conglomerates. If you want to reach a bigger audience, you have to connect with those who are already talking to them. And yes, this may even mean talking to your competition.

Part of marketing is to make your audience aware of why and how much they need your product. If your local or international competitors have done a good job of building a message. Why not joining their efforts? They are already talking about the same topics. They have already caught the audience's attention. All you have to do now is understand where you fit in.

You can always build on the messaging, or the value that will be brought to your audience. That's why it's important for you to know what you bring to the table. Your values become essential once again. You don't want to jump on a trend just because it's "hot". The key is to jump on the right opportunities for YOU. If something feels forced or not aligned, I promise you, it will come back to haunt you if you force it. I've learned this the hard way.

How did collaboration become the new strategy for business?

Influencers and artists have showed us more evidently the power of joining forces. Why not listening to the new single by this new artist that my favorite artist is promoting? Why not watching the show that stars my favorite actor's son or girlfriend? Why not buy that brand that both of my favorite athletes are wearing in their off-time? If you have an audience of 10 thousand followers, and join forces with a different audience with similar behaviors or interests, you may reach hundreds of followers that did not know about you.

Actually, if we had been paying attention, we would have seen that nature has many lessons in collaboration. Just as many, if not more, than in predatory practices and survival of the fittest.

Trees and bugs collaborate all the time. Even different species collaborate to ensure their survival. We focused too much for too long in the predator model. That only leaves some people winning at the top.

Why would we do that? When we can all win bigger and better battles!

Every time I see "Shark Tank", my initial reaction is the same: Fight it! Why would me, a little tiny fish, want to go into the Shark tank to get preyed upon? I don't like the idea of having to pitch your business so that someone else can grow it or benefit from it. But then I switch my perspective into new-business mindset. Yes, you want to be swimming with sharks. Get some benefits from the leftovers they didn't want, catch their draft, learn their ways…

As long as the end-goal is mutual benefit, it's good! And if you can go from 2D to 3D and find a multi-benefit area of opportunity, that's even better!

Collaboration is complicated

I'm not going to lie, it's not easy. Not because it on itself is hard, but because we are not used to it. We live in mostly individualistic environments. We don't want to waste time "explaining ourselves". Even in more community or family-oriented societies, we tend to go with the flow. So, we use broken or obsolete methods, just because they have guided our community, country, family or organization, not because they work.

Collaboration requires the following key elements:

Clarity

- *What does each participant do?*
- *What do they bring to the table?*
- *What are the benefits?*
- *What are the expectations?*

- *Limits or boundaries?*
- *What happens if things go well?*
- *What happens if things go wrong?*

These are just some of the questions that need to be discussed. Clarity can go hand in hand with honesty. But I focus on clarity, because communication is complicated. You can be honestly misunderstood. Your intention can be one, but perceived to be a different one. Sometimes we think we said something that is clear for everyone involved, but it's only clear to us. Sometimes we were distracted, we overlooked, misread, or didn't hear clearly what was said. We're fallible and human!

Make sure that all the terms of your collaboration are clear to you and everyone involved. Run scenarios or tell stories where you can illustrate how the collaboration would play out so that people can ask questions with practical answers. However long it takes you to get clarity, it's time well-spent.

Organization

- *Deadlines*
- *Times*
- *Procedures*
- *Requirements*
- *Tools*

All of this can be coordinated in simple meetings and calls or conversations. But it can grow as complex as entire multi-platform software systems that operate worldwide. You can keep track in a notebook and cross-check every now and then, or hire a project coordinator. The level of complexity may vary, but the principles are the same. You need to know what you're working with, and how things are expected to unfold.

Communication

- *Official communication*
- *Progress-reports*
- *Casual communication, follow-up*

I have mentioned before that I have jumped between industries and jobs. But the core element of all of my work has been collaboration. Whether running a research task force, producing a musical event, or preparing a new online product launch, I'm used to collaborating. And the first, most valuable lesson I learned was how to communicate with my teams.

Official communication includes contracts, agreements, announcements, and big events that everyone has to know.

Progress reports, show people that whatever was planned to happen, did happen. How everything that came together to make something happen worked, or did not work. It gives everyone an indicator of how their work is impacting the final outcome.

But, honestly, the most complex and important of all is casual communication. If you over complicate communication, you end up with email chains with hundreds of emails copied to twenty (or more) people. Or that beautiful meme that says "That meeting that could have been an email." I would even say, that email that could have been a message, or phone call.

How do you determine what kind of communication you need? Well, first you assess your own strengths and needs. Are you visual? Do you learn better by listening? What kind of communication suits you. In which channels? Text messaging? Emails? An online platform?

As with everything else, collaboration will be the result of your personal participation and needs, with everyone else's. You may not end-up getting everything exactly as you wanted it, but make sure that you do have everything you need in order to make things happen.

Collaboration is not about making sacrifices, but about bringing together what everyone needs to thrive.

Online Collaboration

If you do your work on your brand, product, or service, and post it clearly on your online resources, people will easily engage and collaborate with you. Nowadays users know that they can tag, comment, or follow their favorite brands or influencers online. And that is precisely where they show you love. Users collaborate with brands naturally if you just give them the right tools to use.

Your workers, employees, and associates, collaborate with your brand too. Every time they post where they work, and their daily experiences being a part of your team, they are sharing your brand's stories.

If you do a good job offline (product quality, user experience, corporate culture), you will get awesome results online too (followers, reviews, recommendations, mentions). The tools you need to provide others are simply:

Your digital presence (usernames included in your packaging, bio, website, etc.)

Updated spaces (you don't need to post every day, but make sure your logos and branding stay up to date so people can verify your identity.)

Shareable content (create beautiful content that can be useful to your users, not just salesy stuff: A beautiful image for Mother's Day that they would even print and send as a card. Motivational content. Instructional or historical background on things that are important to them and to you. Shout outs to people who make your brand, your community, or your values bigger. If you engage with your community, they will engage back with you.

8. Small Business Does Not Mean Local Business

You are not alone in your process.

You are not the only one feeling pain.

You are not the only one feeling hunger.

You are not the only one who wants to live in a better, more peaceful, more bountiful world.

Talk to "them"

In another zone, in another city, in another country, in another continent, in another culture.

You'll realize they are very much like you.

You are not alone.

You are closer and more similar to "them" than you may have imagined.

You and they can become us.

Bigger, better, us.

Just a click away.

What do you think of when you hear "small business"? A little shop in your neighborhood? Someone who sells home-made goods? A little craft-shop?

Historically, small businesses operated locally. They had under twenty or fifty employees (depends on which standards you use) or they were a one-man (or woman) show. However, technology and social media, changed the way we grow our businesses beyond borders and time zones. Along with the types of businesses, products, and services that could be created in these settings.

Remember when we used to make a big deal about call centers in one country serving people on the other side of the world? What if you found the perfect web designer in a country far far away? What if your best strategic alliance to distribute those handcrafted purses or organic soaps was half way around the world? What if that great craft that took hours and earns you very little money in your local town, becomes a valued art piece in another country?

Small businesses are now capable to connect with other small businesses almost anywhere in the world.

This is generating alliances that help them grow as much as they want to. Entrepreneurs have sized down in growth and operations with less greed than corporate businesses worldwide. Why?

For some soulpreneurs bigger isn't necessarily better.

Don't get me wrong success and growth are still part of the **soulpreneur** mindset. It's just that they come second or third in the list of priorities. First is financial stability, then enough time for personal life and family. And if business is good, and all goes well, they perfect the process. Cheaper, more sustainable, give something back to society or the planet.

Then, when business is GOOD, they go bigger.

What does GOOD business mean to soulpreneurs?

A business that allows those who participate to live happy and healthy lives. Good relationships with one's community, family, environment and business allies are key. If none of that takes place, **soulpreneurs** won't seek to expand their business practices.

Soulpreneurs seek worldwide connections and alliances with people and businesses that align with them. That way the work, pressure, and possible complications, get spread out among a whole team. This means that team work, collaboration, and coordination are a must. And that is what makes technology such a key element in this process. Online collaboration and follow up, allow for great things to happen, at the same time, even miles and miles away.

Our overcorrection: Money is evil.

We tend to see the traditional business model as a very Scrooge, big-polluting corporation, monopoly model. And yes, for the most it is. But, it has created a bit of a money allergy in many of us. What do I mean by that? Well... The assumption that money is evil and rich people are bad. Which, is totally false.

Money, just like any other tool, can be used for good or for bad. And rich people, just like any other people, are imperfect. They can do great things with their resources, regardless of their motivation. And they can also do very bad things with their resources, regardless of their motivation and knowledge of their impact.

We want to do good! We don't want to repeat the same mistakes. And sadly, many of us have said this without a doubt, but great ignorance of what it would bring to us:

"Money isn't important to me."

So then... we have debt. We don't sell our products. We are overworked and underpaid. The money we finally somehow gather seems to slip through our fingers.

Or we'll use phrases like:

"If I didn't have to make a living, I would be happy."

The truth of the matter is that money is our value currency. It helps us mix and match what we do with what we need. Even if we escaped the current currency systems, we'd have to put a value to what we do. N number of hours of my work for N number of items from your garden. Money just simplifies this system. Yes, even to the new generations enamored with cryptocurrencies and NFTs. They are still a way to ascribe value to something. And sometimes, even more arbitrary and impersonal than our current systems.

The general assumption is that people work to make a living. We need to eat, live somewhere, provide for ourselves and our loved ones, use services, etc. Well, you will always have to "make a living", even if you become incredibly rich overnight. You would have to spend your time doing something, even if it's vacationing or playing golf. And you would have to manage what you have, or lose it as easily as it came to you.

The truth is that we don't work to make a living.

We work to put our talents to the service of others.

Whether we clean houses, harvest crops, drive a Formula 1 car, sing a song, produce movies, do research, make organic soaps, sell crystals, or do someone's taxes... Yes, that service and the value we bring through it, gives us something in return.

How do we make peace with it?

Money is an asset. It's useful. It can help us help others. It can help us support the things we believe in. From the music and artists, we like; to the products that we find more useful, humane, practical, etc.

Having more for the sake of more, will always leave you empty.

Even if you're just saying "I wish I had more clients". It may be a good vision for your future. But what will you do with them? And more importantly, what will you do FOR them?

Again... if you can't figure out the value exchange that you have with one customer, you won't value what a hundred, or million customers bring to you. Nor, what you bring to them.

I learned this while working with singers. I could see a great singer being as happy and fulfilled as possible just singing to a room full of friends and family. Yet, miserable and drained after singing to seventy thousand people. And it's not because of it being "commercial". It had little to do with the setting, and a lot to do with the mindset.

Appreciate every bit of value you receive.

Every good review, every cent, every deal you close is great!

Appreciate every bit of value you give.

A new product sold, a new participation on a networking event, being a guest in a podcast, a new post... Everything you bring into the world to make it better!

If you do this, you will see that money becomes just a performance indicator. And it will come more easily to you, because it has a purpose and true value. You are no longer putting resistance to it. You are no longer blocking it away from your life, nor fearful about it going away. It will not hurt you or turn you into the person you're trying NOT to be. You will be the person you WANT to be, thus being able to use money wisely, humanely, and smartly.

9. Boundaries and Putting an End to Discrimination

I do not know what it's like to be you

To live in your skin

To live in your mind

To walk in your path

To suffer your pain

To write your story

But I do know me

I know my mind, my path, my pain, and my story

And I commit to make sure I won't use any of them to destroy, belittle, or dismiss yours.

This is a hot topic, and one that requires a complex and in- depth study when you approach it from a social-justice angle. But all in all, what we need is to treat people with dignity.

Those of us who love deeply, tend to get hurt deeply, right? "Nice" people are thought of as weak, because others take advantage of them. While **soulpreneurs** are deeply human, sensitive, wholehearted and caring, we are not weak. The fact that we approach others from a perspective of honoring them, doesn't mean we will dismiss ourselves or the Higher good.

Soulpreneurs are change makers. And as such, we don't take "status quo" arguments at face value. We are the kind of people who ask "Why?" or "why not?" often. We talk about Higher good, because we don't just take our needs and perspective as rule or law. We build upon our knowledge, and seek diversity in opinions, experience and views.

We dream of better ways to be, live, and enjoy life. But it's not just about being idealistic. We make things happen! Sometimes for good things to take place, the toxic, damaging patterns, relationships and structures have to stop. We know they don't stop on their own, after all we have seen again and again that some of the most tragic events in the world have happened because good people didn't step in to stop them. True love requires setting boundaries and cutting the cycle of abuse, exploitation and discrimination.

Dignity is not just for a group or class. Dignity is available for everyone, because it doesn't cost a thing. Treating people with dignity is a choice. And not just people, living beings and creation as a whole. Even if you'll end up eating that chicken, there are many ways for that to happen. Happy open-range or polluted and crowded wet market? If you work in a big corporation because you HAVE TO, you can make sure that everything that happens under your watch, adheres to the dignity you would seek for yourself.

Setting boundaries may feel odd at first. We are naturally wired to seek the approval and appreciation of others. We are not so naturally wired to disagree with others, or to let them know kindly and peacefully that there is another approach to what they do or believe.

Have you felt rude or cruel when confronting someone regarding their discriminating attitudes or practices?

Let me share with you an experience of my own. A couple of years ago, I was working a multi-disciplinary project. There were many of us there, some with advanced degrees, some fresh out of school, and some others who may or may not have finished high-school.

Regardless of our background and preparation, we were all crucial to the success of the project. Team work was demanded, not an option, an obligation. Basic activities like driving, cleaning, and keeping the workplace in order and running properly were just as essential as communicating with people worldwide, using computers, and high-tech resources.

But we're human right? We seem to take every opportunity we have to share our trauma. Do you think car drivers are lazy? Do you think rich people are entitled? Do you think young people don't know what they're doing? Do you think older people can't use technology? Well, mix all of that with stress, and you'll get the perfect storm.

Long hours... Many things in stake... I understand we are probably not all at our best. Not our best behavior, not our best patience, and definitely it does not lead to our best manners. So, what happens? We blame each other. And we start with the basics: "That was so simple, how could he miss it?"

Then we move to: "He obviously wasn't ready. He is so lazy!" And eventually we start throwing biases and discrimination:

"That's just how *those* people are you know?"

Before you know it, instructions become commands. Requests gradually turn into yelled orders. And we don't see it. We just think everything is "fair game" because we are under a lot of stress and the task must take place. Boundaries are gone!

How about that? We allow, endure, and encourage this "authority" or "leadership roles" even when we are destroying all decency and humanity for the sake of a project. And it doesn't stop… it leads to mistreatment, insults, and loss of decency and dignity. All it takes is for people to remain quiet for the sake of a paycheck, or to avoid conflict.

Some say that's just the way it is, right? But we're **soulpreneurs**, we know better! Under stress, we can shift and stir away from blame. We can come together knowing we are all facing the same stress, but we want the same goals to be achieved. Success can happen for all of us by coming together. We can figure out what the "other" needs to do what we all need them to do. I can think for a second and find what it is I need to do better or more of for all of us to do better.

How do you feel about it?

We have normalized cruelty as a way to enforce the rules of the game, or keep "control" of a project. Even though, most of us honestly despise people who attempt to "control" us.

Soulpreneurs understand stress, but we know that no outcome justifies the loss of dignity. Every team-member demands and deserves the same respect. If you would not feel good about your client or boss yelling at you any command, then you shouldn't do it to those people working under your command.

You can enforce rules. You may also demand respect for the workplace and other team-members. Sometimes you may even have to speak up, stop someone's behavior, language, or step out of a room to show that what they're doing is not ok. You may have to step into that zone that you would usually consider "cruel" in order to let kindness win. Boundaries, remember?

There is no other way to break the cycle, other than acting according to our values. ALWAYS.

No exceptions allowed.

Boundaries are easily stated and shared if you have learned about collaboration. Stating expectations, rules and regulations clearly, helps you uphold them, keeping everyone accountable for what they sign-up for. Boundaries help you achieve the task, without losing dignity.

You can't play the game if you don't know the rules.

This is the dirty little secret that makes dictators cringe when you talk about improving education systems around the world. This is the excuse for discrimination that people have used since the beginning of time.

I have struggled for years watching all sorts of injustice all over the world. From poor people used as tokens in every political campaign, to workers in a factory being used as a negotiation token of a dispute they will never win. Frustrated workers being fired from their company because of "globalization" or down-sizing. In all of these instances, the players have no idea of the rules of the game. They don't know that sometimes "losing" is actually winning, when you have all the information at hand. They also don't know when they are being played, because the boss doesn't give you a choice.

In my area of expertise, I can tell you that **Economics** is a game with plenty of simple rules. **Business** is the profitable part of that game. **Marketing** is the cool branch of that game. And **digital marketing** is the little playful toddler that loves shifting the game.

Why do I focus on these 4 elements when I talk to soulpreneurs?

Economics is the name of the game. It brings together everything we are and everything we have to play with. Our talents, our vision, our skills, our resources, relationships, etc. It uses those funny little tokens we usually call money. It has the basic premise that someone has what someone else needs.

You can choose whatever system you want to use. Capitalism, Marxism, Liberalism, and any mix of those. Each system may make everyone benefit in different ranges, different levels of individual freedom, collective organization, etc. It really doesn't matter how you organize it, in the end someone needs what someone else has, and vice versa. Even the wealthiest and most centralized system, needs the "little guy or gal" to do something for them to enjoy it.

In any and all economic systems, businesses will happen. Businesses are needed to keep things going. Whether we talk about entrepreneurs working together in an eco-friendly sustainable manner from home, or sweatshops in the worst conditions under the toughest dictatorial regime.

Even in nature, bees need to pollinate flowers, and they need flowers to nurture themselves. Predators need to keep control of populations, and they need to feed, themselves and others. Different value interactions are needed and will happen, and someone will get something out of it. The difference may be how that benefit is distributed and supplied.

Marketing is how you tell the world of the existence of your business. That's just it! It's your love letter to your dream customer. It is also your way to say "I'm here to play the game and become part of the system". How will you play it? As a disruptor maybe? As another block of a smooth-running chain? Whichever you choose to be, you are still a part of it.

Digital marketing, is the online version of this. In many ways digital technology has been a world-wide equalizer to say "I'm here". But it does not mean you have to rely on it for your existence. You don't NEED digital marketing to become or sustain a business. But you really want to learn how to use it so that your voice will be heard in ways that you may not be able to make it heard in the physical world. It can close the gap between you, your clients, and allies. It can also become a new enslavement and disparity tool.

It's not the system, it's how we use it.

Not "against", but "for"

Soulpreneurs are not the people who fight against injustice. We work, fight, operate and build towards justice. We don't fight discrimination, we make everything needed so that we make room for inclusion. We don't tackle ignorance, we educate through inspiration and interaction.

It is very easy to get caught up in resistance. Don't get me wrong, there was a time in humanity's history when resistance was all that minorities, oppressed, and underprivileged people could do. In my experience, that is not the case anymore.

Many people believe in revolution and radical changes. I am not one of them. At least not in the "burn down the house" way. I believe radical changes and revolutions are not long-lasting. Furthermore, they have way too many casualties and they just perpetuate hatred and disparity. That said, I do believe a radical revolution is possible. The kind that is built in such a way that the whole system shifts for good. But, it doesn't happen overnight.

How do you achieve true progress and change? It doesn't happen unless you seek win-win options for everyone. Obviously, when there is a group in control of everything, they won't enjoy conceding. But, just as I mentioned previously in the book, win-win options are more available and abundant than we think.

For example: If you tell a rich person that paying better wages to their employees will actually improve their own living standards, they may not agree with you. But, if you build a successful business and prove to your peers that everyone is better off because you are paying higher wages, providing opportunities and supporting your local communities you already shifted the system. No need to convince others that you're right and they're wrong. Just walk the talk. The outcome shows itself.

So, don't complain about the things you deem unfair or unjust. Change the system through your actions. Change starts and prevails when it comes from you. If you believe in peace and prosperity, start putting it to practice. First within yourself, the way you talk to yourself, the way you spend your time and resources. Then move a step further, with how you treat those closer to you. You can't preach peace when you can't treat your brother, your mother or neighbor with respect.

Experience, enjoy, repeat in a bigger setting. That's it!

And yes, this may include public service and politics. That is not out of the question, that is a part of the system we can't forget about. Whenever I talk about community, this may include your neighborhood, your business, your country or the world!

It is not good vs. evil

We do need to acknowledge that we are all capable of good and evil deeds. We make mistakes, and even deeper, we can sin. Whatever "sin" means for you, it's a deeper and more painful impact that we have on others through our actions. It's ok. We do not have perfect knowledge. Even when we have good intentions, we may fall short.

That said, if you continue to judge, blame, and "fight" the "other", the journey will be long and tiresome. Acknowledging our humanity is key. Everyone's humanity. Not just the one of those you love and respect. As a matter of fact, it is particularly essential that we admit the humanity of those who wrong us. None of us is below the "other".

You may be more familiar with the term "compassion". That is what we really need wherever we become caught in conflict or wrongdoing. That doesn't mean that you will endure things and behaviors that are destructive. It does not mean that the culprits get to walk away. For sure, it does not mean that there is no accountability for those who have caused pain.

Our behavior cannot become rash, violent, or vindictive just because "others" have done us wrong. The key here, is what happens with us? Hatred doesn't affect those who have wronged us, it harms us. Feel it in your body. That strong anger against someone who has really caused pain in your life.

We all need to heal. The victims and the perpetrators. I have seen it and experienced. That is why I keep writing "others" in quotation marks. Because there are no "others", even if we are very different and we may live far away from each other. We are all connected in many ways. And we can all be the victim and the perpetrator given the chance.

I have been attacked by people who have been victims of violence themselves. I have been attacked with racist slurs by people who have been wronged by racists. I have been attacked by women for standing up for women. It is not a judgement, it's a reality. Just like I have attacked others when I've felt hurt. When we claim justice and forget about the healing behind it, we are in risk of becoming the perpetrators.

It is not an easy process. As a society we are not all ready to go there yet. We are barely listening to the stories. Some of us are just finding out how much harm we have done. Some others are just learning that while they thought they were victims, they were actually the ones doing harm. Humanity is barely learning how inhumanly it has behaved. It is quite the reality shock!

However, one step at a time. One person, one story, one action… We can move closer to justice, and dare to go into healing so that we stop the cycle of pain.

10. Bigger and better business

So much to say

So much to do

So much to learn

So much to prove

May my growth help others grow

May my success inspire others to bloom

May my strength support the ones around me

May my Light help others see a better path

Is bigger and better your next step? Many of us are trying to make our business grow, but what does this mean?

One of the main reasons to make our businesses grow is our desire to earn more. That is fine, living a comfortable life is good! You want to take that trip you have been postponing. Or maybe you want to upgrade your business tools, your car, your office, etc. A new baby in the house? Moving out of that apartment and building your dream home? Paying off debt?

Once your business is working and you are doing ok, you want to do better. So bigger and better is maybe unavoidable. It is just the next step, but how do you take it without losing sense of what worked for you?

We are all creating monsters.

We are all creating monsters even if we do not know it, and we too have the power to make them disappear. If you are feeling slightly overwhelmed these days with all the craziness in the world and you really don't know what you can do about it. That is precisely the reason I am sharing this.

We are so powerful. We have more tools, resources, and information than ever before. All of this is power in our hands. Every action we take adds up to millions of other people taking a stand for what they want and believe in. What we do, say, and choose matters.

I'll let you in on a little secret that Mark Zuckerberg, Steve Jobs, and Jeff Bezos didn't know. And if they did, they chose not to pay attention to it. They didn't sit in their dorm-room or garage or tiny office and think: "One day I will be super rich with this project and I will mess up the world with it".

Zuckerberg didn't say: "One day I will be hacked and have millions of users complaining about their safety. And I'll have to testify before congress and the European authorities because they used my 'popularity' algorithm to mess up with local elections."

Jobs didn't say "One day my phone will pollute the world because everyone will keep buying the newest model and throwing the other one in the trash. And it will be super expensive even if it doesn't work better than the last model."

Bezos didn't say: "I will kill small businesses and local shops everywhere, and pollute the world with all the trash my packing will include."

The secret is that they didn't see it coming. Just like Coca-Cola didn't start bottling their product to become one of the world's biggest polluter. Coal miners didn't choose coal just so that it would create unbreathable air, and Marie Curie didn't intend for radiation to be used in the next best weapon of mass destruction and cancer-creating element. That IS a fact.

This is what I call the Frankenstein Phenomenon, and many of us take part in it when we create something.

Anywhere from songs, to businesses, and technology, we have been taught to create whatever we CAN. Nothing is impossible. We can make anything happen. And so, we develop programs, content, businesses, products, applications, platforms, and such. However, in this process we rarely stop and think:

What if this works?

What if this is a success?

We spend so much time figuring out how to make it work, that we leave little to no room to what happens when it does. So once the monster is alive... If it causes trouble, if it destroys something, if it hurts someone... We claim we didn't know it could happen. How could we, right? This was new. No one had ever thought of dealing with this problem, because it didn't exist.

So, we started using fossil fuels, and didn't think the whole world would be polluted, warmer, and destroyed by them or for their sake. We created plastic and never thought that it would kill nature and end up in the ocean, and much less back in our system while eating the same fish who ate it. We composed songs with hate speech demeaning women, minorities or promoting hate and violence, and thought they were just fun. It isn't like people are going to listen to them all day or take them seriously, right?

We created digital platforms that connected the whole world, where people would trust us with their personal information, but could not imagine someone would misuse them. We created clothes, and gadgets and told everyone they needed "the newest" and "the latest", but did not plan for when they disposed all of them. Right? We created a world focused on making more money to spend in more things, but rarely did we stop to think what it would make people feel, believe or behave. Or did we?

Did we know better?

Did we choose to look away because it was too uncomfortable to face our responsibility?

If we didn't know better then, we do know now, and we can do better.

The truth is, we now know this, and we cannot look away anymore:

The newest iPhone is trash.
Yes, the newest iPhone, and that pair of shoes, and the container and bags you're disposing after using them for a couple of minutes. If we know that everything we produce, can, and will eventually, become trash. What will we do about it?

Facebook is Frankenstein on the loose.
Facebook is Frankenstein on the loose, beyond its makers control. And when you have a monster on the loose, you do not make the monster bigger. You focus on what it needs to operate safely.

The content we create can be our own monster.
You see everywhere that you need to "feed" the algorithm. Post "n" times a week. But what is that content doing? Is it providing value? Is it feeding your ego? Is it compensating for your lack of self-esteem? Is it just "crowding" your timeline? Every piece of digital content that we are creating has to be stored somewhere. Do you know where it is stored? Do you know it heats up the machines where it's stored and that's why they put it underwater? How much does it cost? How much does it cost our environment?

Progress has a cost.
Every time something new comes up, it replaces something old. How do we prepare for it? Who will lose? What opportunities will come from it? Are new tools and skills needed? Are we developing them? Are we giving an option to the people who will lose, to find a way back into the system where they can win?

Are we doomed?

I'm not against progress. Sometimes tough choices must be made. There are needs that we have to fulfill, and remember we mentioned dignity? Housing, clean water, access to electricity, connectivity, etc. Those things sometimes imply pollution, expansion of urban areas, etc. Even when those things need to happen, I hope we make our priority to reduce the impact of progress on our natural environment. For now, every step in the direction of progress seems to be a step away from something else.

The most important part of this process is to learn how to make the tough choices. To become more creative and resourceful as a collective of human beings, to find better solutions to all of our problems. Having more informed and sensitive leaders who understand the cost of choosing one option over the other. As well as the need to stop having to choose between A and B, and maybe come up with hybrid options that turn out to be ABCD altogether in one. Less negative impact to all the parties involved, and more positive impact for the global communities.

Now we know that we are creating monsters. We cannot say 'nobody told me' or 'I didn't see it coming'. Even if you're innovating from scratch, and no one has ever thought about doing what you're doing. You know! If you stop for a couple of minutes and analyze what you're doing, you will see it. That project you're developing or that thing you're creating.

Who is it going to hurt and who will benefit from it?

It does not necessarily mean that you stop yourself from creating or innovating. It just means you have to step up to the challenge, and know what you're causing. If it will hurt someone or something in the beginning, and it is unavoidable... Then...

How will you make it better?

What will be the first step you'll take to make sure it helps more than it hurts?

What steps or actions can you take in order to help those that will be hurt by it?

If you want to learn more about the Frankenstein Phenomenon and other ways in which our innovative and tech-loaded mindsets have shaped our reality, please read my book **"Caught In Between".

I can tell you that before growing your services or the size of your workforce or equipment, you have to get better. Is there something in your process or services that could be done better?

BETTER:

- *Less waste*
- *Improving working conditions*
- *Developing new skills*
- *Creating opportunities*
- *Healthier lifestyle*
- *Improving mental, emotional, and physical health*
- *Less pollution*
- *Obeying local and international regulations and standards*
- *Safe environments*

- *Holistic approach*
- *Cultural development*
- *Positive social impact*
- *Diversity and inclusion*

Maybe you're not great at keeping all projects on track. Maybe your quality control is too complex. Whatever may be less than great in your business, I recommend you take a look at it before contemplating growth. Trust me, if you get bigger before getting better at it, you will suffer. The size of your business magnifies the size of your problems. It will become harder to focus on those details as you grow.

Is there a point where big is too big?

Assuming I'm talking to you and you are not Jeff Bezos, Carlos Slim, Dietrich Mateschitz, Leonardo Del Vecchio or a shareholder in one of those Unilever, Bayer, Nestlé companies... you may be far from this point. But yes, for everyone, there is always a point where big is too big.

When the work in your hands goes beyond the hours that you were planning on devoting to it. It is too big. When the number of tasks go beyond the number of people who can perform them, it is too big. When you cannot take care of the quality and the content you're putting into the world. It's too big.

This does not mean you have to stop growing. It just means you need to find what can close the gap. Growth must be strategic and intentional. And, above all, it must be connected to whatever can keep your business happy, prosperous, productive, and efficient.

Wanting more impact, more income, bigger communities, more products, that's all good. It wouldn't be normal to expect a business owner who has the drive to change the world, to just "settle". But the size of your business has more to do with what you can provide in value, and less with your greed or vanity or need to conquer or demonstrate your glory.

The ideal size of your business.

Is there such a thing? I think so, even if it's just the right size for now. Bigger and better can go hand in hand. Better should take the lead in your focus, because it may bring you more value even before you decide to grow. Almost unavoidably, doing things better will help you grow your business. It will make you more appealing, and more valuable to clients and investors.

However, going back to the ideal size of your business. That is whichever size will allow you to:

Pay attention to each customer.

Know who they are, what they need, and keep track of their progress. If you are losing track of them, or find yourself rushing through reports or conversations, you may want to get better at this, before growing more. Don't get me wrong, it doesn't have to be YOU keeping track of them, but anyone in your business should be able to find this information.

Pay attention to each supplier or coworker.

As with customers, make sure you are keeping track of them, their progress, and the time and attention you devote to them.

Once again, this does not mean that the owner, or manager should be able to know all of this, but that they will be able to find this information and use it as easy as possible.

Do no harm.

If any part of your process is causing trouble anyone involved with your business, you may need to reconsider the size of your business.

Again, this goes with bigger and better. If your business growth did not consider in the process the people, community, and resources that make it big, you need to go back.

If your impact to society, the local economy, or natural resources is negative, then do something about it. There is always a way to make any process better.

If the impact is overworked people, then get creative with schedules, roles, or think about new skills or hiring. If the impact is that you outsourced to a cheap provider that is not being animal-friendly, then change your provider or work with them to develop better procedures.

Getting bigger and better sometimes includes helping others become so too! Growing other businesses and becoming part of their investors, management team, or council can be a good opportunity for personal growth. It may not involve your whole business, or it might.

The world needs bigger and better businesses, but bigger not in terms of size or income.

We need businesses that have bigger purpose, bigger vision, and community development.

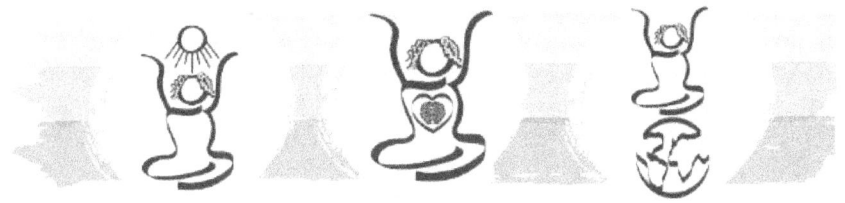

11. Three Reasons to Make LOVE the Core of Your Business

Losing yourself to win more than you could imagine

Overcoming your fears with your inner strength

Valuing yourself, and everything that surrounds you

Expanding your capacity to be, become, and achieve everything all the time

The understanding of your origin, your place, and your perfect interaction with everything and everyone around you.

That is love, you are love, all is love, denying it is just a waste of love.

Let me share with you a little bit of my story and my commitment. I, like many **soulpreneurs**, am in the business of love.

I love business. I have mentioned my education in Management and Economics, and since I practice what I preach, I studied what I loved. Numbers make me happy. However, my education taught me to go beyond, and make sure that I knew what numbers stood for.

I know that numbers represent the people who benefit from something, or the income that will allow them to house and feed their kids. Percentages are not empty figures, they show the people who respond or need something, or those who don't. Numbers represent progress, results, opportunities, and possibilities.

Numbers are a symbolic representation of effort, passion, imagination, need, skills, and they can be the reflection of love. So, they will matter, even when you make love the core of your business. But they're no longer the goal, they're just a representation.

Loving business?

Yes! I strive to help people love their business. Loving the time they spend "at work", and the people they work with and work for.

In my daily activities oftentimes, I have to remind my clients to enjoy their process. Whether it is the fun creating process for their products and services, or the nasty business-y tech side. Numbers, analytics, taxes, and business set-up are somewhat overwhelming for many soulpreneurs and creatives. But that does not mean we need to stay away from them.

We need to understand that each and every business activity enables the good, fun, powerful side of our business. Don't get rid of the nasty, understand it, and embrace it as part of your process. If all else fails, you can always outsource to someone who actually enjoys doing it.

The universe is so perfect that you will always find someone who enjoys doing that thing you simply cannot stand doing. Yes, some of us actually enjoy the numbers, analytics, and other business-y things. But do not disregard it or let go of it completely. You are still in charge of your own process, even if someone helps you with it.

Spreading love through your business

We are living in a world that puts profit first, and that is not an entirely bad thing. A business that turns no profits, won't live long. Nonetheless, putting people, well-being, happiness, and environment protection as priorities is way better. And you will find that, you cannot take care of the people, happiness, and nature without making a profit.

When you really want to make a difference in the world you need to get creative. Now more than ever before, we are understanding that what we do in our daily lives has positive and negative impact in our communities and surroundings.

Some of us no longer justify those negative and destructive behaviors as a necessary evil, because we know better. You do not have to work 15-hours a day to make money, you can find more productive and positive ways to work 8 to 10 hours, or less, while feeling proud of it and living with ease.

Always think about how someone can benefit from what you do. In everything you do!

Your attitude matters. If you're serving others at a restaurant and put the right attitude behind it, you'll get better tips. You will listen to what your customers need. Maybe suggest things that you know they will enjoy. Then you will make sure to check on how they are finding their food, and think of something else they may enjoy, a refill, desert, etc.

If you are a lawyer, you can put love into the time you devote helping your client, and go above and beyond for them to feel safe, supported, and understood.

If you are a health coach, you will check in and keep an eye on your client's progress. Maybe you'll share some content that your client needs or values? Maybe you care for them as people, and not just focus on the project's goals?

There are many ways to spread love in your business beyond donating to charity or organizing tree-planting festivals. More often than not, the own business or project's reason for being can have an additional human connection or opportunities for growth and connection.

It's now or never

I can tell you that if you are planning on coming into the business of love, now is the perfect time. Have you seen the news? Have you heard people in the streets and how they talk or feel? I have said it before and I will say it again. Even if some don't believe it:

It is profitable to do the right thing.

Though it may not be as quick and easy, it is profitable. It too may take longer, and it may require more effort and collaboration, but it can be done. Angry people are not as productive. Frustrated people make more mistakes and take more time doing things. Happy people are productive. Productivity is good for business! Loving people make businesses more welcoming, and will have more customers returning than those who simply care about a paycheck.

There are many digital and creative resources to get you into the business of love. Spreading love, inspiring love, and working with and through love. It's not cheesy, it is really becoming a case of do or die.

I'm choosing "do". How about you?

Some inspiring stories from others who have chosen to make love the core of their lives and businesses:

I'm sharing this special section of the book with the words and brief stories of people from all over the world who are working with love as their focus. Even if they don't identify themselves as soulpreneurs, they are people worldwide who have walked their own journey.

They are real. They have wins, and tough moments. They are part of different industries, and projects. They are great reminders for you to know that you're not alone while trying to change the world. For every person, or event that shows you that things are going "wrong", you can find stories like these, of people who are trying to make it better.

"My purpose is to live with more intention and help others do the same. I chose to live off grid and on a bus conversion in part, so I could live more consciously in alignment with my values of Earth care, people care and social justice.

There is no greater joy for me than feeling that alignment and seeing my values expressed in the choices I make every day. Even the most menial task like doing the dishes can become a soulful and intentional practice.

Of course, there are days when it's tough. Living intentionally doesn't mean living easy. But I simply return to my values, all of the things I appreciate and working towards this lifestyle is a no brainer! Living in alignment can be challenging, but living out of alignment was painful."

Sarah Taylor,
International Business Coach, Ethical marketing & strategy,
South East QLD, Australia.

"I have 18 years of business experience in the e-commerce space, and yet being the CEO of a startup that sells software for spiritual-minded professionals, while having little kids, is a new landscape I have to keep re-learning how to navigate. I'm one of the fortunate ones who has a husband that willingly participates in handling half of the kids 'stuff,' and even then the juggling act of both of our careers and very empathic children is challenging. During the over a year that the COVID pandemic has been a factor, this daily grind can become mind-numbing at times, if I don't remind myself hourly of my Why.

I show up every single day because of my kids. Because of your kids. Because of your nieces and nephews, or children you see in your neighborhood. Because in my mind's eye my goal is to knock over a bunch of dominoes until they start a revolution.

My company makes it easier for healers and spiritual-minded professionals to share their talents with the world. In turn we hope they'll help heal A LOT of people. And of those people many will be parents, who will be open to the idea of helping their children heal from a young age. Can you imagine whole generations of kids that get to adulthood without the baggage most Millennials and earlier generations can claim?

They'd create a beautiful world to live in. Checkmate. We ALL win. But winning involves a lot of clarity, direction and effort. So when the days are blending together and I can't bear to have even one more thought… I stop. I nurture myself.

I sleep.
I dance.
I read fiction.
I paint (horribly).
Sing the parts of a song I can actually remember.
I love on myself.
And reconnect with my spirit.

So I can do the hard inner work of staying in integrity with my values everyday. Of being present with my children. Of having clear boundaries with people. Of creating a workspace that's creative and supportive for my team.

Because I know slowing down will help me speed up, and work from a place of Flow. And because I know who I have to be, and at what vibration, for the Universe to support my vision for the world. That person is a calm and empathic leader with a lot of foresight, and a mother with a lot of patience. And neither is easy without giving myself a chance to pause and recalibrate.

So here's to loving yourself…so you can show up in the world at your highest potential. Because I know you have some talents to share too that could help heal the world."

Simran Bhatia,
CEO Flowation
Chicago, USA

"I'm sure you know the saying the saying 'move from love, not fear'? My business has given me - or to be more precise, my heart - a practical experience of what that means.

In my work of supporting women embody their conscious being and leading from it, it's important I stay in my heart and in a space of love more often than not. Otherwise my guidance is flawed by fear, or hijacked by stress - and that's not how one passes on wisdom! When I'm deep in my being, it's almost like a permission slip to my clients to safely explore their own inner landscape.

That said, easier said than done! Us humans are complex creatures, and our cyclical nature plus the multiple dimensions of being require acute awareness to understand what supports me to be at my best in any given day. Routines, like meditation, movement, journaling and breath, give me great solace & foundation but I've also grown conscious not to use them as a crutch. Hence, the more I understand myself, the more I also appreciate slowing down, the rest, and the occasional treat as I can see the impact of that to my wellbeing. Sometimes the most self-loving thing is a nap!

Something that's been resonating with me lately is the idea to plant seeds every day, rather than putting the focus on harvesting. We are after instant results in today's Western lifestyles that I'm committed - rather than self-inducing anxiety - to focus on great quality work & presence on the daily and to cultivate trust that with time, it is rewarded. I feel this gives me a better chance to live in alignment with what I care about - and in the end, this is what really matters."

Anna Kuusela
Embodiment coach for conscious female leaders, dancer & yogi and an adventurous spirit from Finland

"I create music because I have come to acknowledge that creating uplifting music is my purpose in life. I started it as a hobby but later I realized that was it was much deeper than that. I had an uncle who was a musician who passed away when I was very young. Some of my earliest memories include watching him play an 'Orutu," a traditional one-stringed instrument amongst the Luo tribe of Kenya. He also played the guitar. He loved music and had vivid visions that he would describe to people of playing his music all over the world. He died young and didn't get to realize even a fraction of his dream because poverty and its effects devoured his aspirations and his life.

I often get this feeling that his dream is being lived on through me. As an independent musician I go through a lot of struggles but it's the love for music and the belief in it that keeps me going whenever I feel disillusioned. The music is not about me, it's for everybody, it's a legacy. It was there before me and my purpose, my passion, my love is bringing it out to the world."

Nixon Omollo

Musician, Kenya

12. Popularity, Impact, and Transcendence.

You are made of star dust
The material of the Universe
Even if you're just a speck of dust
You are made of Divine Light
Filled with the same power that makes seeds grow,
stars shine,
living creatures breathe,
and mountains stand.
You are perfection
in connection, in awareness, in integrity.
I am too.
They are too.
You are special, but not more special.
You are essential, but not more essential.
You hold perfection and embody perfection, even when you are not perfect.

We live in a daily popularity contest. How many followers do you have? How many people love you? What do you see as your success? The number in your bank statement? Even the most spiritual of us tend to stumble and fall here.

Trying to find outside, what can only be found within. But... we have the inner desire for transcendence. That is very different from popularity.

Many business coaches and strategists make a living with marketing statements around "Building a 6-figure business", or how to "Build your list" or "Grow your business". Is that wrong? Not really, there's nothing wrong with wanting to do better, and sometimes those statements help us summarize our vision of "better".

But is it what is best for us? Does summarizing success in such ways keep us honest about our purpose? As I've said before, bigger is not always better. Having 100 clients may just multiply your number of problems, not your fulfillment. Making more money may not be really the best outcome for your work. Ever heard: "more money, more problems"? This can be true, or false, it's not about the money.

However, when your purpose is clear, and your energy is aligned, having 100 clients means that you're making an impact in the world making those 100 people happier, healthier, more fulfilled, etc. It will also lead for that energy to seek expansion. More people to impact, more spaces to show up, more ideas to promote, and so on. It could be 100 bigger clients, or more projects with those 100 clients, or just an ongoing relationship and deeper impact with just 10 clients.

Soulpreneurs are change-makers

Soulpreneurs are chasing a vision of happiness, fulfilment, evolution, progress, etc. That makes us radical change makers. As I mentioned before, we are not people "against" what's wrong in the world. We are individuals that make "good" grow.

This also means, we usually don't want to build on the status quo. As a matter of fact, we are major disruptors. We want to break it all down, or like a game of Jenga, take the pieces that aren't needed, one by one without making it all fall down. There's no one way, or one style with us. But, chances are that we are too sensitive to want anyone or anything to get hurt in the process.

And so, we either tip-toe around our goals, or we bring down the house. We tip-toe if we are too worried of how our actions will impact others. We rattle the whole thing, when we see things are too broken, painful, and harmful to stay as they are. The commonality seems to be that we do want things to be better, and are willing make them happen.

If you're thinking: "Doesn't everyone want things to be better?" I am very sorry, and quite troubled, to tell you I've found this is not true. People may want things to be better with the traditional old-mindset standards; but wanting things to be BETTER for the Highest Good of everyone involved isn't necessarily the trend yet.

If you feel like you are finding more and more people around who DO want what's best for everyone... GOOD! Hold on to that vision for dear life! And keep your focus on those who can help you stay in that lane. Chances are that's why you found this book. Your vision of GOOD and BETTER is needed, and you are helping build it.

You help to build it by noticing the people around you who may be like-minded. You help to build it by believing that it is possible and defending it to continue to be possible for yourself and others. There may be times where you lose track of your path, or overwhelm and stress make you a little bit less hopeful about this. It happens. But your vision of what is possible, can be real. Don't give it up.

What is your impact?

It should be clear by now that every one of our actions and choices has an impact on our lives and other people's lives. What we think, feel, and do will shape everything around us. Yet, as we go through life, we forget about this.

I remember growing up, I used to collect tons of letters and gifts from my friends. I still have many of them! Boxes of stories, compliments, drawings, and little reminders of people I loved, and who loved me back. When I went to college in the United States, I took some of them with me. A couple of notebooks with messages from my High School friends, the best letters from my closest friends, and special items my family had given to me. All of those things reminded me of how much they loved me.

When I felt down or homesick I used to read them. Sometimes it was a VERY bad idea, my mind twisted it into "You'll never find this here... Look what you left behind!" But, other times, I understood an additional value to all of those letters and things. Many of those letters and messages included "I'll never forget how you helped me with...", "This year wouldn't have been the same without you.", "I'll miss you".

Those quotes and lines are testimony of people who changed me and were changed by me. When I felt little or uncapable, they allowed me to see that I was important to someone and I could achieve things. I was loved. I was special to someone.

Now, as I look back in my life, my words, my actions, and my presence have impacted thousands of people. Nothing to do with the followers in my social media account. Not as a popularity contest of how many people signed my yearbook. But noticing the number of people that I've worked with, and just shared a moment in my life.

Think about it yourself. Start with your inner circle. Your family and closest friends. Who are they? Make a quick list. Now, think about the people you grew up with. Cousins, neighbors, peers... Again, make a lit. Now, look back. Who was your family and your inner circle 5 years ago? 10? 20? Add them up. Now, imagine that each one of them has impacted roughly a similar number of people. Chances are something you did for them, impacted not only them, but someone around them.

That sandwich you split with a friend during recess because they forgot their lunch... Maybe it helped them keep a positive attitude that stopped them from getting into a fight at school. Maybe it allowed their brain to learn better so they could get a better grade. That impacted them, and maybe others in your classroom or school. Maybe it made their mom or dad proud of the grade they got, or gave them peace of mind because they thought their kid hadn't eaten. Perhaps it showed them that someone cared for them at school, giving them joy.

That is impact! And yes, as you move into the world of social media, the impact you have may go bigger and broader than you can keep track of. But it goes beyond how many followers you have, and how many likes you get. You could just have ten followers, and you can brighten their day with a quote or a photo. You could educate them about something they had never heard of. You could even convince them to take action on something valuable at a global scale. Just ten people, right?

Maybe in an audience of 1,000 you get someone to just see your message as they scroll down. But the words stick to their minds just enough to help them figure out something they were struggling with. No likes, no comments, just impact. Isn't that wonderful!?

Now look at it from a different perspective. You get to 200,000 followers in your social media account. You have 3,000 subscribers in your newsletter. You have sold 10,000 units of your product. But... You've just been going through the motion to make your "list grow". You have no connection with them. You are posting messages that "sell" but don't reflect who you are. You have no connection with the people who follow. How does that feel? What does that do for you and to you?

Yes, we want YOU to make a big impact. More than that, my wish is that no matter the size of your impact, whatever you do has a BIG impact in YOUR happiness, fulfillment, and growth. Just keep in mind, your impact may be unmeasurable, and it may not come in the shape, form, or channel you may have expected or planned.

Using your platform

Working with artists, I got to see very often that they had lost their "self" and their purpose, as popularity came along. Some of them would step into venues with thousands of people and just feel burdened. They would only worry that they would fail, or just go in and out of the stage as if nothing had happened.

On the other hand, I can tell you the beauty of the exchange that happens when an artist values the audience. When artists come on stage with their game "on", in sync with their staff and musicians, and wanting to share their joy, talent, and gifts with the audience, the outcome is magical. And everyone involved in it can feel it.

My favorite moment working with pop artists was when they sang their big hit. You know that ONE song. The new single that was playing on every radio station. The first song they promoted. Their big fun song. The one power ballad that just gets everyone singing and or calling someone on the phone. It usually happens near the end. The worry of all of us making things happen is gone by then. And the song comes up. You can feel the energy of the audience flowing all over the stage and backstage. You can feel the energy of the artist flowing all over the venue. And if the artist stops singing and the audience takes over... WOW! The magic is complete.

I chose this moment, because it's the most evident and present outcome of impact I have witnessed. I have also seen it with influential people who have changed someone's life with a book, a quote, some advice. It happened to me once in college with someone who heard me speak in a local TV interview. I had never met this person, I didn't know anyone would watch that show, and I got a very powerful letter telling me what it had meant to them that day.

You never know who's watching or listening.

But when it is soulful, it is powerful.

Even though it was public life, celebrities, and influencers who allowed me to see the impact we have on people. Your platform can be way simpler and apparently smaller than theirs. Your platform could be your sidewalk or the lobby of your building as you interact with your neighbours. It could be your office-space, the phone calls you make, and the meetings you take. It could also be your social media, a podcast, or a blog.

Now, don't fall for the trap of playing a part just because people are watching. Be who you are, and be mindful of your impact. But remember, the most important member of your audience is yourself. How do you feel about yourself with how you act and behave? Be compassionate, don't demand too much of your imperfect work-in-progress self. But do know that you are powerful, and the changes you make in the world, matter. They add up, with mine, and everyone else's.

Years from now, you can look back and see how your actions were part of a bigger change. Sometimes it's obvious, sometimes it takes a little more looking around. I myself have seen that little actions I took ten or twenty years ago, contributed to big actions today. I can also see the impact that other people had on me, and others like me. Things a teacher said, the friendship someone shared with me and others. That project that inspired people to devote themselves to artistry, or social work, or entrepreneurship. That is how we transcend.

Beyond popularity and fame, it is not that one action, it is the collection of events, ideas, actions, and relationships that we form throughout our lifetimes. That collection shapes others, and the world around us. It can be as simple as that thing that you do just like your grandma did, or your best friend. It can be as complex as the technology and tools you use every day.

13. Let Go of Your Fear and Flow from Love

Stop looking around
Start looking within
Darkness, noise, and chaos fade out
Your Light shines brighter
Your heart sounds and feels stronger

Most of the choices we make every day tend to be loaded with a pack of fear. And that is precisely what's been pushing us to make tougher and tougher decisions. From politics to our daily decisions. What should I do? Where should I go? Should I mention that this procedure is not complying with regulations even if it means doing it all over again?

Well... are you doing it because you're afraid of what will happen if you do? Or if you don't? How about doing it because you care for others, like and enjoy what you're doing?

The truth is that your choices may very well be the same. The options you may have can actually be the same as well. But, that said, operating from fear gets you stuck, frustrated and limited in more ways than one.

Flowing from love may sound like a radically naïve concept. However, it is all but naïve. It takes a lot of courage.

I've talked before about love economics, and how love changes the approach and the outcome of our actions. But when we talk about our decision-making process it becomes key! Most of all, because we are naturally wired to operate in "survival mode", and that is based out of fear. Nowadays, we have evolved enough to switch out from it, and operate from a new mindset. Oddly enough, it is the new key to our survival: love.

What does it look like to operate from fear?

When you make a choice operating from fear, your thoughts are based on avoiding danger. You may choose to work, because of the fear of not making money, getting fired, or missing out on a promotion. Fear of being perceived as a failure, not smart or capable enough, or not being accepted in the professional environment of your choosing. It's like a hunter going out for a prey, because otherwise they will die of hunger. Or getting married for the fear of living and dying alone. Can you see where this is going?

Operating from fear usually leads to rushed decisions, settling, frustration, not to mention general paranoia.

Overall, not the best and more efficient outcome is expected. You may end up living without the best use of your time, skills, and resources as a whole. Even putting aside that you are not going to be happy, fulfilled, and you may never feel "safe", it's just not efficient. If it's not efficient, it's not good for the economy. So, whether you're a practical being, or a soul-centered person, it's not the best choice!

Switching It Up and Flowing from Love.

Let's got back to the exact same scenarios we stated before, but switching them to the love flow.

You may now choose to go to work, because you enjoy what you do and you feel useful. Anything you leave behind to make it happen won't burden you, because you feel it's worth it, and your overall attitude will be positive. You go to work to make good use of your skills, to contribute to humanity, to make the world a better or safer place, etc.

A hunter going out for a pray because it allows them to practice their skills and bring a meal for their community, may enjoy the thrill of the hunt and make a full outing of it.

A person choosing to get married because they love the other person and want to build a joint life, a family, and shared life projects poses a very different outcome from the one we mentioned before.

I talk about flow, because **soulpreneurs** tend to be people who try to do everything great, and that usually means we put a lot of effort into things. Sometimes, that means that we make simple things, more complicated than we should.

I have a wonderful peer and friend who has worked deeply with the concept of flow in business. I really like and have integrated her views into my own path and process. I think this is a very powerful tool for **soulpreneurs** who are trying to let go of fear, failure, and resistance. This is one of my favorite quotes on flow from her content and conversations:

> *"Instead of fighting, you want to flow. Instead of overwhelm, you want to create. Instead of stressing, you want to expand.*

*You crave change, growth, and that is natural within you.
You are energy in constant movement and expansion.*

Flowing is opening yourself to possibilities, but this can only happen if you are willing to cope with uncertainty. And that is where true difficulty resides, at least at first. The need to keep things under control is a very deeply rooted thought. But, just like all other thoughts, it can be replaced."

Paula Acuña

Flowing from love leads to a better economy.

I always come back to the efficiency and balance that love brings to a free capitalist-based economy. And I do focus on a capitalist economy, because it's the most widely spread and used in our planet. Flow brings up efficiency because we are making the best use of our resources. Our energy, emotions, and thoughts are resources as well.

Just like an algorithm, each of our choices is feeding the economic system. If you believe in a universal or divine system where good deeds and positive energy are compensated, then you are feeding that system too. Every thought we think, every action we perform, every relationship we build shows the system what we stand for.

When we show in our daily behavior and choices that we would rather live a healthy life, than a sugar-loaded carb-based diet, the market responds! Likewise, when we feed the system that we would rather work in a job we love, live in a healthy space, and share our lives with people who make us better... Guess what? The world responds! It's not just energetic, Law of Attraction stuff. Even though it is energy-based attraction. This is just a basic use of Supply and Demand. We are the Demand for a better, cleaner, wiser use of our resources. That includes dignity, health, balance, nourishment, happiness, and many other things.

Lightening the load, helps you operate better.

It's actually pretty basic. If you're not afraid, frustrated, or overwhelmed, your brain can focus on other things rather than just keeping you alive. You are better able to create, imagine, analyze, focus, etc.

That way, little by little, just like your load is lighter, so is the world's. If more of us flow from love, as opposed to operating from fear, there are less harmful scenarios for all of us.

If you don't believe me, try it! Just for one day. Every choice you make, see where it's coming from. Just ask yourself why am I choosing to do this? And if you find yourself thinking "I don't have a choice", then take another step back and see how you got into that position. Chances are that "I don't have a choice" moment, comes from a traumatic event in your life. Catching yourself in that moment, may be a great opportunity for growth and healing. Take it!

And remember:

You may end up making the same exact decision, but your intention and your focus make a difference!

Final thoughts.

If you don't believe me, try it! Just for one day. Every choice you make, see where it's coming from. Just ask yourself why am I choosing to do this? And if you find yourself thinking "I don't have a choice", then take another step back and see how you got into that position. Chances are that "I don't have a choice" moment, comes from a traumatic event in your life. Catching yourself in that moment, may be a great opportunity for growth and healing. Take it!

I want to make sure you understand that this is not magical thinking. Things don't usually change overnight. However, when your mindset, your approach, and your motivation changes, your experience of reality changes too. You are better able to see opportunities, and the good in the world. You are drawn to people who live lives more similar to yours. But don't forget to look around.

Just because your reality has changed, it doesn't mean that the world around you has all of its problems solved. Be kind to others. Be mindful that some problems are greater than your immediate solutions. But do not let that make you feel like you are not doing enough. Continue to make one choice at a time. Improve your life, do what you can to improve the lives of those around you, and keep your eyes open for opportunities to "level up" and serve bigger and higher communities and causes.

The time will come, don't hesitate, you ARE the right person for that job. And when it does, remember that you are not alone.

www.ingramcontent.com/pod-product-compliance
Lightning Source LLC
Chambersburg PA
CBHW070426220526
45466CB00004B/1563